Biblical v. Secular Ethics
The Conflict

Biblical v. Secular Ethics

The Conflict

edited by
R. Joseph Hoffmann
and Gerald A. Larue

PROMETHEUS BOOKS
Buffalo, New York

To the Memory of
Joseph Blau
(1909–1986)

Published 1988 by Prometheus Books
700 East Amherst Street, Buffalo, New York 14215

Library of Congress Catalog Card Number: 88-61000
ISBN 0-87975-418-4

Printed in the United States of America

Contents

6   Contents

PART TWO: RELIGIOUS ETHICS AND
HUMANIST ALTERNATIVES

Preface

R. Joseph Hoffmann

The use of the Bible as a standard against which to measure the rightness or wrongness of human action is a well-established custom in Western societies. Disputes ranging from high school debating contests to Supreme Court cases have been won and lost by appeals to a text whose uniqueness and authority is often assumed to be self-evident to "moral" and right-thinking people. Increasingly, however, society is outdistancing its ancient literary comrade. As the race between technology and human values poses unprecedented questions concerning the criteria of "moral" action, the Bible cannot help but show its roots in the tribal and customary laws of the ancient Near East.

We may lament the fact that the early quest for justice, equity, and national identity reflected in the chapters of the Old Testament, or the "love ethic" often ascribed to Jesus in the New, are thus rooted in unfamiliar ground: Western societies, after all, have grown up with the Bible. Constitutions, statutes, and ideas of government—ranging from absolute monarchy to representative democracy—are thought (sometimes wrongly) to be derived from its mandates. It is impossible to think of a Shakespeare or a Goethe or an Eliot—or indeed an Isaac Newton or a Spinoza—without the continuing conversation between the Bible and the cultures that have hosted it over the centuries. Yet Western society, as it continues to respond to a rather different set of cultural demands than existed in the Middle Ages and in the Renaissance, finds it harder and harder to accommodate its old friend: A book that teaches the inferiority of women, the permissibility of slavery, the ostracism of non-Jews (and later, non-Christians), the stoning of disobedient sons, the necessity of blood-feud and vengeance, and a dozen

7

other unsavory attitudes and rules, scarcely qualifies as an instrument of intellectual and social liberation. Those who have tried to make it so—those who espouse the social theology of the secular marketplace and who despise the marketplace as a retailer of wickedness—have managed to show only that in the 1980s one can salvage but bits and pieces of The Book or offer up niceties drawn from its parts as the whole of the Judeo-Christian message. What becomes clear to the unbaptized as the century draws to a close is that the baptized have begun to use the book merely as a hammer for political views, denominational moral dicta, and religious propaganda. To say that there is nothing new about the abuse of Western culture's ancient literary friend in this manner is an obvious thing; but one may lament, along with its passing from the scene, that it must die in the disgraceful circumstances to which its loving friends have reduced it. Were there Shakespeares, Goethes, and Arnolds to save it, or Spinozas to redeem it—like Job from the rubble—the culture would not, as it now must, bear the guilt for making it look ridiculous at its going out.

The Bible was once an instrument of enlightenment. It was the book upon which the monastic and artistic culture of the Middle Ages thrived; the book that inspired men of brilliance and accomplishment from the third century onward. In harder circumstances after the Renaissance, it yet remained the patient adversary of the *philosophes* and finally the fuel for naturalist and rationalistic philosophies well into the present centuries. Its defenders among the Christian people have ordinarily been shortsighted, not only about its history but also about its virtues; as defenders of its literal "truth" they have sided not with the true legates of the prophets, scribes, and teachers—not with the Jeremiahs and Pauls—but with the Philistines. In defending the ethics of the Bible as the revealed and unchanging word of God, they have made God a creature of the past and his word a dead note sounded to an unhearing people who knew not Joseph. As the Bible was the lifeblood of humanism and humanist ethics, as it engaged the imagination and demanded new responses to changed circumstances, so fundamentalism and its cousins have been the Bible's deathblow.

The essays collected in this volume recognize the importance and antiquity of the Bible's contribution to moral discourse. Their authors cannot be said to represent any single-minded position on the question of the "validity" or "truth" of biblical ethics, but many of them would agree that the moral world view of the Bible belongs to the period

1500 B.C.E.–100 C.E. and thus cannot and should not be thoughtlessly invoked to settle moral questions. Many would argue that the Bible thus used is misused: that to seek the "will" of God concerning abortion, birth control, capital punishment, apartheid, social equality, human rights, or the rights of women in biblical writings is to revert to the law and predelections of the tribe as a solution for our moral curiosity. Most of the contributors argue some form of the thesis that biblical ethics are not "normative" but "situational," that is, the ethical views of biblical writers are grounded in the moral concerns of their own day and their advice and opinions, including even the *soi disant* Ten Commandments, are caught in the relativity of time, place, and circumstance. At least some—certainly not all—of the authors represented in this volume will suggest that biblical ethics are irrelevant, or potentially irrelevant, in making the hard moral choices that "modern" society demands of its members. However, in arguing what may seem an unfriendly thesis, most would agree that this irrelevance does not entail the notion that the Bible has nothing to say about ethics. On the contrary, what it has to say may inspire fruitful reflection and even more humane solutions than the ancient text itself proposes.

This volume represents the second in a series produced under the auspices of the Committee for the Scientific Examination of Religion and its Biblical Criticism Research Project. The committee is the leading collaborative effort of its kind in North America, bringing together on a regular basis international experts in the fields of biblical and religious studies (including archaeology, textual criticism, and history) and their cognate disciplines. The purpose of the committee, since the time of its founding, has been to bring forth for public inspection and discussion the very best in serious, nonparochial biblical and religious studies scholarship. With this volume we come somewhat nearer that goal.

Introduction

Gerald A. Larue

Once again the Committee for the Scientific Examination of Religion (CSER) presents a collection of essays that challenges current concepts and evokes reflection and re-evaluation of traditional notions. The first volume in the series, *Jesus in History and Myth* (Prometheus Books, 1986) incorporated papers read at the First International Symposium held in April, 1985 at The University of Michigan, Ann Arbor, under the auspices of the CSER subcommittee on Biblical Criticism. The present volume is composed of papers read at the second such congress, which was held at the University of Richmond, Virginia, in 1986. Once again, outstanding scholars were present, including Theodor H. Gaster, Morton Smith, Joseph Fletcher, John Priest, Richard L. Rubenstein and the late Professor Joseph Blau. Indeed, several of these men were honored with special awards in recognition of their magnificent contributions to scholarship (Professors Blau, Fletcher, Gaster, and Smith).

Each paper in this collection calls for deep consideration of issues pertaining to biblical ethics. For example, Professor Eakin roots present-day anti-Semitism in the New Testament and, through a careful analysis of key texts, he projects the hope that ancient divisive concepts might be bridged to provide "meaningful association" in the present—certainly an expression of the humanist vision. Professor Hoffmann, co-editor of this volume, challenges the idea that the New Testament can serve as a source book for ethics.

This book, like the first volume in the series, is composed of the work of experts but is designed for the thinking nonprofessional. The intrusion into our homes by the voices of televangelists and other clergy has popularized numerous clichés about biblical ethics. These insistent

11

voices, when not asking for money, appear to base their claims on a handful of biblical verses lifted out of context rather than on contextual analysis of biblical concepts. The resulting encouragement of noncritical Bible reading produces followers who are both naive and truly confused in their understanding of the scriptures. Such nonevaluative reading is challenged in the present group of essays. As passage after passage and book after book is analyzed, new and clearer insights emerge. The question arises: How can the Bible be viewed as a source of Jewish or Christian ethics?

One can only wonder at those who claim to read the Bible from "cover to cover" and who state that they find espoused within these books the highest ethical principles. Obviously they must read without comprehension, for from its very beginning in the book of Genesis the Bible portrays both the deity and its central heroes as liars. The lies may be deceit practiced for expediency, but the results are lies nonetheless.

When Yahweh created man (Adam) in the "J" creation myth (Gen. 2:4b-3:24), the deity obviously wanted a nonthinking creature who, like an animal, could be trained to obey. The first efforts to produce companions for this first person resulted in a massive clay-rolling-and-shaping exercise that brought forth "every beast of the field and every bird of the air," each of which was given a name by the man-creature, and none of which satisfied his needs or desires. Finally, Yahweh produced a woman (Eve) who was fashioned from a rib extracted from the man. Adam had been warned by the deity that although he could eat fruit from the trees of the garden, the fruit of the tree of the knowledge of good and evil was off limits. Indeed, the man was told "in the day you eat of it, you will die."

This threat was a lie, for when the man ate he did not die. The lie was one of expediency, as the serpent, who was somewhat wiser than the man, explained. Yahweh knew that eating of this wondrous tree would raise humans above the animal status by providing awareness of, and the potential for judging, good and evil, which Yahweh had reserved for heavenly creatures alone. This "truth" was confirmed by Yahweh after he became aware that his command had been violated. As the serpent had promised, the humans did not die; and Yahweh admitted, "Lo, the man has become like one of us, knowing good and evil . . . ." The serpent told the truth; Yahweh lied. Now, inasmuch as only one thing separated humans from the acquisition of full divinity—immortality—Adam and Eve were expelled from the sacred precincts "lest he put forth his hand and take also of the tree of life, and eat, and live forever. . . ."

How can those who turn to the Bible for ethical principles fail to recognize divine deceitfulness? Does the fact that Yahweh lied justify the lie of expediency? But then some of the early Bible heroes were liars as well. Abraham lied. He told King Abimelech that Sarah was not his wife but his sister (Gen. 20). But perhaps this was only a half-lie since Sarah was his half-sister. He spoke the same lie to the Pharaoh of Egypt, thus permitting his wife to become part of the Egyptian royal harem (Gen. 12). Abraham's son Isaac lied in exactly the same way with respect to his wife, Rebekah (Gen. 26), and she in turn lied to Isaac as she conspired with her son Jacob to rob her first-born, Esau, of his birthright by disguising Jacob as Esau to the confused, half-blind, and dying Isaac (Gen. 27). Indeed, Sarah lied to Yahweh when she denied laughing (Gen. 18: 9-15).

One does not need to be a biblical scholar to recognize deceit and dishonesty no matter how it might be explained away. To accept the lie of expendiency as a moral standard would provide justification for deception in religion and government, as recent public exposés of the PTL (Praise the Lord) group and the Iran-Contra scandals have. In both instances men of high office confess their Christian beliefs in public but have been shown to make use of the "lie of expediency."

As the pious reader wades through the convoluted ethics of the Bible to the tortuous visions of the author of the book of the Revelations of John, principles of mercy, love, justice, and forgiveness fade away, while the anger, hostility, retribution, unforgiving judgment, and harsh punishment that exceeds the crime tend to dominate. Consequently, only the few righteous believers among the earth's billions are deemed acceptable.

What is the humanist response? The first essays in this volume deal with the biblical ethic and the problems associated with efforts to proclaim it as the source of the highest principles to guide human action. Is the lie of expediency to be included? Does the Christian ethic embrace cruel vengeance as portrayed in the harsh, unforgiving father-God image? Is such an image the model for human parenting? Most Jews and Christians ignore these portrayals: they stress justice, peace, goodwill, love, and human understanding, but they arrive at these lofty principles by way of the process of careful selection. It is issues such as these that occupy the first part of this important volume.

In Part Two, the nature and content of the humanist alternative dominates. Here the appeal is to sources beyond the Bible—philosophy, history, great minds—all representing the human quest for values. Of course the Bible is not excluded but rather treated as the product of groups of humans who lived in the Palestinian world some 2,000 to 3,000 years ago. Selectivity is involved because there is no claim of divine absolutism. The humanist ethic recognizes human fallibility: it is aware of the variations in human thinking that emerge and evolve through social and historical changes. It continues to enhance the democratic principles of free thought, free expression, and the centrality of that which is human—both male and female—in evolving the highest human ethic.

Part One

Biblical Ethics and Contemporary Morality

1

Biblical Ethics and Continuing Interpretation

Gerald A. Larue

No informed person will question the impact of the Bible on the development of life and thought in the Western world. Indeed, nearly one half of the world's population—including Jews, Christians, and Muslims—honor the Bible either wholly or in part. Its themes appear in great art, great music, and great literature. Our everyday speech is sprinkled with phrases rooted in the Bible: one escapes by the "skin of his teeth" (cf. Job 19:20); goes "the second mile" (cf. Matt. 5:41); sees "the handwriting on the wall" (cf. Dan. 5:25), or any of a variety of phrases that have found their way into the vernacular.[1] Numerous kind and charitable programs are rooted in biblical teaching. There can be no challenge to the obvious: many good and decent persons, families, and groups root their humanitarianism and high principles in biblical precepts.

Our present concern is with biblical ethics, with those who would make biblical moral teachings the law of the land, and with those who would compel their neighbors—near and far—to adhere to particularistic or denominational interpretations of the Bible. They would lock today's ethical standards into the thoughts and beliefs of those who some 2,000 to 3,000 years ago lived in a small corner of the Mediterranean world. On the basis of their unquestioning faith, they would bind us to the ethical edicts of generations past: the long-dead would control and inhibit the living.

Gerald A. Larue is professor emeritus of archaeology and biblical studies at the University of California at Los Angeles.

But none of these "true-believers" really accepts all biblical teachings. There is a pick-and-choose principle at work that enables each group to determine which moral, ethical, or ritual requirements are essential for acceptable life and conduct and which may safely be ignored. For example most Christian groups believe that Jewish ritual laws, including those for testing the validity of charges of adultery (Num. 5:11-28) or proving the virginity of a new bride (Deut. 22:13-21), are irrelevant; but there have been some Christian groups who called for the killing of homosexuals, basing their arguments on biblical law (Lev. 20:13).

Ethical codes and moral teachings tend to reflect communal norms. As communities change in size, compositon, in life-settings and outlook, norms also become transformed. At the present moment, we have no way of knowing just how our earliest ancestors established communal patterns. Perhaps there was rule by the strongest, in which case might determined right. Perhaps, as some have suggested, a primitive democracy was developed through which decisions were made by vote of the free men of the commune.[2] By the time we get written records from the ancient Near East, we encounter established codes of conduct that are undergirded by the authority and power of the church and the state. The regulations are said to have been provided by one god or another. The enforcer of these rules, the king, who was not only the projected embodiment of the state[3] but also recognized as the god's chosen vassal, worked together with the established church and the temple functionaries to maintain the divinely established order. Through ritual, myth, and sacrifice, state religions underscored the authority of the revealed law and supported the monarch as the divinely ordained maintainer of the holy precepts. At the same time, the religious functionaries secured their own positions as servants of the gods and as divinely appointed interpreters of myth, ritual, and religious precept.[4]

Divine ordinances defined the topocosm[5] or place-world of the particular group and, in so doing, gave the group identity as people of a particular deity who share a common life, a common purpose (which was to serve and exalt the deity[6]) and a common means of fulfilling the divine prerogatives. The codes, designed to define, promote, and maintain harmonious relationships within the community, specified both acceptable and unacceptable behavior. Conformity to the prescribed norms ensured divine blessing; deviance resulted in punishment.

The various moral codes of which we are aware prove not to be the creations of individual rulers. They reveal direct borrowing or dependency upon accepted practices current throughout the ancient Near

Eastern world. The famous seventeenth-century B.C.E. law code of King Hammurabi of Babylon reveals affinities with the earlier codes of the nineteenth-century B.C.E. ruler Lipit Ishtar of Isin, and with the twenty-first-century B.C.E. code of King Ur Nammu of Ur.[7] But each of these codes claimed a unique and divine origin. Ur Nammu's laws came from Utu, the Sumerian sun god; Lipit Ishtar's from Enlil, the wind god; and Hammurabi's from Shamash, the Babylonian sun god. When biblical law was established, it, too, borrowed from current codes and common practices and, like its predecessors, claimed divine authority given by the Hebrew god Yahweh (Exod. 20ff.).

Hebrew scripture teaches that the Jews are the chosen people of their god and that they are in a covenant relationship—a formal, legal compact—with him in which Yahweh agrees to be their god and they agree to be his people (e.g., Deut. 14:2). As in other such arrangements, the chief purpose of the people was to serve their god so that he in turn might reward them with rich blessings—a pattern that could be classified as *do ut des:* I give so that thou mayest give. The acceptable rules of conduct, which embraced everything from ethical principles to proper sacrifices and acceptable food, were disclosed to Moses in a personal encounter with Yahweh on the top of sacred Mount Sinai (or Horeb). At a later date, Yahweh continued to reveal his will through his prophets—at least until the time when Jewish savants decided that all prophecy had ceased.

A similar pattern prevails in Christianity. The Jewish notion of covenant was retained, but the Mosaic or "old" covenant was superseded by a "new" covenant. The new lawgiver was Jesus, who had no need to consult with the deity, because he, like the Egyptian pharaohs, was god incarnate—god-in-human-flesh—living among his people and revealing his divine rules.

Now ethical codes either bind and inhibit human life or liberate and free individuals, enabling them to maximize their human potential. Restrictive, inflexible regulations fit into a category labeled by Joseph Fletcher as "rule ethics." Those precepts that exhibit flexibility without encouraging anarchy or complacency or indifference to human rights while enabling ethical principles to be interpreted with regard to unique or particular human situations or contexts, Fletcher labels "situation ethics."[8] These categories have significance for our understanding of biblical ethics.

CONTINUING INTERPRETATION IN THE JEWISH TRADITION

By the fourth century B.C.E., the Jews had sanctified the Torah as *the* holy revelation. All other "revelations"—all Jewish scripture—had to conform to this ultimate truth. When discussions concerning the content of the Jewish canon ensued at Jamnia (Jabneh), Israel, about the end of the first century of the Common Era, some Jewish writings were challenged on the basis of nonconformity. For example, the writing ascribed to the prophet Ezekiel was questioned because it conflicted in certain places with the Torah (e.g., Ezek. 46:6 and Num. 28:11). It is reported that a certain Hannaniah ben Garon, laboring night and day and burning 300 barrels of oil in the process, harmonized the discrepancies. He was able to prove that when Ezekiel contradicted the Torah, he really did not contradict that sacred work! The "Song of Songs" was admitted to the Jewish canon as an allegory of God's love for Israel. Thus, when the lover states that the maiden's shapely thighs are like jewels formed by a master hand and her lower abdomen (vulva) is a round goblet not lacking in wine (7:1-2), the reader is to understand that this is a reference to Yahweh pouring out love for his people Israel, and not some lovesick Jewish swain's description of his sweetheart. The principles at work in the acceptance of certain controversial writings into the canon included reinterpretation and allegorization.[9]

But long before the first century C.E., Jewish savants had engaged in a process I have called "continuing interpretation."[10] I refer here to the fact that once precepts were accepted as divine utterances, the religious community was stuck with them, in much the same way that the Roman Catholic Church is stuck with *ex cathedra* papal utterances. But times and life-settings change, and what once appeared as a pertinent and fixed regulation no longer fits precisely into the new situation. Somehow the divinely revealed commandments must be kept but provided with a new interpretation. It was not possible for Jews to do what the Mormon Church did when the rising tide of social consciousness gave recognition to the black people in America and made Mormon doctrine concerning the lesser status of blacks an embarrassment: simply receive a new divine revelation that admitted blacks into the fellowship.[11] The study of the Jewish Torah discloses a different pattern at work— the principles of continuing interpretation.

Modern scholarship has made clear the fact that the first five books of the Bible, the Jewish Torah or Law, are not the work of a single individual named Moses. They constitute a composite, and there is solid evidence of editing and re-editing that has taken place between the tenth and the fourth centuries B.C.E. For example, when Jewish religious thought moved beyond the primitive tenth-century B.C.E. Adam and Eve creation myth (Gen. 2:4b–3:24), Jewish priests, having been exposed to the Babylonian creation mythology, simply added what is now Genesis 1:1–2:4a. In effect these sixth century B.C.E. priestly writers signed their contribution with the name of the legendary lawgiver, Moses, and it became part of the accepted Mosaic revelation. The new material served to effect a reinterpretation of the older material.[12]

When child sacrifice, which had been called for in Exodus 22:29, became unacceptable to the Jews, this divinely revealed law was conditioned by the insertion of a regulation calling for the substitution of an animal for a child. The new law was inserted into the established code at Exodus 13:12–15 so that it would be read before Exodus 22:29, thereby providing the older law with a new meaning.[13] Indeed, whole bodies of legislation were inserted into the existing law and attributed to Moses, as in the case of the so-called "Holiness Code" of Leviticus 17–26.

During the sixth-century B.C.E. exile, the gloomy, doom-filled oracles of the eighth-century prophets (Amos, Hosea, Micah, Isaiah) were altered. Predictions of hope and recovery of national identity were inserted into and added onto their prophecies. The altered works were then presented as if they were the original writings of the particular prophet. It is clear that throughout the developmental period of the Jewish scriptures, despite the attribution of individual writings to specific inspired individuals, the principle of continuing interpretation was at work. Unidentified contributors, who may or may not have claimed to be inspired, altered older writings, omitting wherever feasible, inserting where statements could not be easily altered, and adding new material to change old meanings.

Reinterpretations did not cease with the closing of the canon. One need only look the talmudic debates to discover rabbinic expositions that gave varying meanings to scriptural injunctions. The pattern extends into modern times and is represented in Jewish sects that extend from Orthodox through Conservative, Reform, Reconstructionist, and on into Humanistic Judaism.

CONTINUING INTERPRETATION IN THE CHRISTIAN TRADITION

The same process of continuing interpretation can be discerned in the Christian approach to the Bible. In some respects, Christian scriptures are a reinterpretation of Jewish convenant precepts, inasmuch as Jesus is reported to have stated that he did not come to abolish the Law (Matt. 5:17). For developing Christianity, the new faith was both a reinterpretation of Jewish thought and a moving-away-from Judaism.

When the Christian canon was developing, there were debates over which Christian writings were to be accepted as divinely inspired and authoritative. Some early materials, such as the Shepherd of Hermas, were rejected; others, like Second and Third John were admitted into the canon only after much debate.

The present-day "search for the historical Jesus" has made clear that accurate information about who Jesus may have been and what he taught has been lost to us. The mist-enshrouded figure that has emerged from modern historical and literary research is too vague and too fragmented to provide even the most elementary personality identity. The numerous "lives of Jesus" are no longer relevant. They are religious fiction, just as the portrayal of Jesus in Christian scripture is, for the most part, religious fiction that reflects the ancient literary patterns employed for depicting hero figures.[14]

The sayings attributed to Jesus by early Christian writers continue to undergo critical scrutiny by scholars. Recently a consortium has attempted to reach agreement about which sayings might be attributed to Jesus and which should be recognized as early church creations placed in Jesus' mouth by the gospel writers. Each saying will be voted upon by the group. Just how much serious consideration will be given to such efforts by the Christian community can only be a matter of speculation. Much of what is under discussion is not new. Clergy trained in modern seminaries have been acquainted with the major aspects of this kind of research. What is clear is that these same educated clergy have not shared their findings with their congregations; thus, in most churches, congregations are biblically illiterate. A great many parishioners believe that they have in Christian scriptures divinely revealed truths and that the words attributed to Jesus have a divine authority that demands both attention and obedience. What they do not know is that the New Testament, like the Old Testament, is a compendium of human writings reflecting the ethical concepts of small groups of people living in a remote corner of the ancient, Near Eastern world.

These writings have no more divinity or sacred authority than any other writings from the same time and period. Both Jewish and Christian scriptures are human products that have been declared "divine" by human councils.

The Gospels reveal the continuing interpretation of Jesus as a hero figure in the early church. New situations were created, new sayings were attributed to him, and new interpretations of his role as the Messiah were offered as the church continued to grow and develop. This pattern parallels the continuing development of Jewish hero figures found in Hebrew scriptures. Aaron, the model of the high priest, and Moses, the lawgiver, underwent continuing changes. Their roles were expanded. New sayings were put in their mouths.[15] As the life-settings of ancient Jews and Christians underwent change over time, the representations of their respective hero-figures changed, too. One can trace the extension of this pattern outside the canon of scriptures. Jewish heroes were exalted in the Apocrypha and Pseudepigrapha. Noncanonical wonder stories about Jesus can be found in the Apocryphal New Testament.

There is evidence of continuing interpretation within present-day Christian communities. For example, some congregations belonging to the Church of Christ, which claims to be the New Testament Church, tend to ignore Jewish scriptures. They focus only on the New Testament. Some of their churches will not permit the use of organs or pianos in their churches because there is no biblical evidence to indicate that Jesus used such instruments. On the other hand, some churches of this same denomination are located in desert country and employ air-conditioning machinery, a convenience that was certainly not a part of Jesus' world. This comfort-giving machinery is admitted on the basis of "expediency." Other Christian churches, among them the Roman Catholic, which would also claim to be New Testament churches, accept as authoritative the Jewish scriptures plus the Apocrypha. Roman Catholicism continues to interpret biblical ethics through various papal pronouncements. Some fundamentalist Christians work in the spirit of Rabbi Hananiah ben Garon, seeking to harmonize biblical creation mythology with modern science by reading into the ancient texts (eisogesis) concepts that are derived from present-day scientific inquiry. Some appear to accept biblical morality; others are willing to admit that they choose what is to be accepted as relevant for modern congregations.

THE MODERN INTERPRETATION OF BIBLICAL ETHICS

There are radical fundamentalists who, in fulfillment of the requirements of Leviticus 20:13, would like to put homosexuals to death. Indeed, there are some who have stated that Acquired Immune Deficiency Syndrome (AIDS) is God's attempt to do just that, despite the fact that the ailment has been spread through infected blood to children and other nonhomosexuals. Other Christians would set aside this harsh biblical sentence of death in favor of teachings about love and brotherhood and would accept homosexuals as children of God and as members of their religious group. Still other Christians have sought to reinterpret biblical statements about homosexuality and suggest that when the Bible appears to condemn homosexuality, in reality it does nothing of the kind.[16]

Some Christian groups take Jesus' teaching about divorce (Mark 10:10–11; Matt. 5:32; Luke 16:18) as important for Christian life (e.g., Roman Catholicism); other Christians simply ignore the teachings because they know that, inasmuch as approximately 50 percent of all marriages end in divorce and that many divorced persons remarry, to emphasize these ancient New Testament notions would decimate their congregations and seriously affect the income of their churches.

Certain Christian groups (e.g., Jehovah's Witnesses) insist that the wife should be subject to her husband's will, as the New Testament commands (Eph. 5:24; Col. 3:18; 1 Peter 3:1), while other groups find it wise to interpret such teachings and to conform to the modern recognition of the justice of equal rights for women. Biblical passages pertaining the status of women are interpreted by still other Christians to suggest that the patriarchal male Yahweh possesses female characteristics (often to the point of becoming hermaphroditic) thus paralleling the great He-She of Egyptian theology or the god Atum of Heliopolis.[17] Various Jewish congregations will accept female rabbis, and some Christian denominations will ordain females; but Orthodox Jews and Roman Catholic Christians balk at this elevation of women. There is, they tell us, nothing in biblical teachings to endorse such a practice.

Some Christian groups follow the teachings in Proverbs (13:24) that a child must be disciplined with physical punishment. Others would agree with the teachings of Ben Sira, whose words are included in the scriptures of the Roman Catholic and Eastern Orthodox churches to the effect that "He who loves his son will whip him often that he may rejoice at the way he turned out" (Sirach 30:1). It is not surprising to learn that church-sponsored schools often employ severe physical discipline, sanctified by scripture of course, and many are the horror stories that students relate from their school days. In many states where physical punishment in public schools has been forbidden by law, church-related schools continue to employ it and escape legal prosecution on the basis of the separation of church and state.

The examples of varied interpretations of biblical teachings and the ways in which they are utilized in modern contexts could certainly be expanded. But it is enough to note that in each instance the Bible is accepted as a divinely revealed rule book—the supreme source for ethical and moral guidance—and that the principle of continuing interpretation is employed so that those who have moved beyond the limitations of biblical ethics can continue to use the Bible as a reference book.

It is important to remember that for many individuals the Bible provides "the way, the truth and the life" (John 14:6). Following the precepts they select from it, these believers live good, decent lives: expressing love and concern for their families, friends, and the less fortunate. Their personal satisfaction in life is increased to the extent they are able to live in harmony with their understanding of biblical morality. These individuals support the synagogue, the church, and the clergy who interpret their scriptures. No attempt is made to compel others to live according to their dogmas, although they may bear witness to these beliefs at appropriate times.

But there are others—most particularly the loud, evangelical fundamentalist groups—who would compel us to live according to their particular interpretations of biblical ethics. They threaten the freedom of dissenters by seeking to have their ethic become the law of the land. Such a law could not satisfy those who believe that humans can live good, decent lives without reference to ancient, antiquated biblical codes, or those who stand for the right of all persons to seek their highest potential insofar as that development does not infringe on the freedoms of, or do harm to, others. At present these fundamentalists seek ways to compel judicial and governmental authorities to conform to their interpretation of biblical ethics. They threaten the personal freedom of all who do not accept their theology, and they assail open and free inquiry as a threat to their interpretation of education, even to the point of compelling public schools to teach only that which conforms to their understanding of the Bible. These fundamentalist Christians would turn back the clock of ethical development to the time of the Bible, in much the same way that fundamentalist Muslim theology has attempted to turn back life in Iran to the time of Mohammed. How do we confront their claims?

The Bible is a part of our Western culture, and only through the honest, open analysis of these ancient writings in the light of the best information available from archaeology, history, comparative religion, and cultural studies can we understand the particular settings out of which its many parts came, and appreciate the various stages of interpretation through which its ideas have passed. Just because some groups claim that the Bible is divinely revealed, there is no more call to accept their claims than there is to accept the identical authority given by some to the Koran, the Book of Mormon, and similar writings. Indeed, each must be subjected to the highest and best critical study available to humans for evaluating the validity of any assertion: i.e., consistency, the scientific method of inquiry, logic, and so on. Our best studies indicate that the Bible is a human creation characterized by differences and contradictory attitudes that one would expect to find in a literary collection produced over a one-thousand-year period. Like any other human work—including the Koran, the Book of Mormon, and other holy books—it reflects the human concerns of its authors and their times. The ethical standards set forth are situational and they reveal that during the millennium that stretched between the time of Solomon (the tenth century B.C.E.) and the that of Jesus (the first century C.E.) the normal, natural, human process of continuing interpretation was at work.

NOTES

1. Roland Bartel with James S. Ackerman and Thayer S. Warshaw have demonstrated the rich contribution of the Bible in literature in *Biblical Images in Literature* (New York: Abingdon, 1975).

2. Thorkild Jacobsen, "Primitive Democracy in Mesopotamia," *Journal of Near Eastern Studies* 2 (1943): 159 ff.

3. In a democratic society such as the United States, the projected image is "Uncle Sam" and on posters urging military enlistment it is the top-hatted, white-bearded Uncle Sam who calls young men to service.

4. The pattern can be observed in present-day religious organizations—the clergy are "called" to their ministry to become interpreters of "the Word," leaders of ritual, and spokespersons for morality.

5. The term "topocosm" was coined by Theodor H. Gaster in *Thespis, Ritual Myth and Drama in the Ancient Near East* (New York: Henry Schuman, 1950), p. 4; (Harper Torchbook edition, 1961), p. 24.

6. The purpose of human life is expressed clearly in *'enuma elish,* Tablet VI, lines 5-9, and this same purpose has been stated over and over again. In modern times it can be found in the Roman Catholic Baltimore Catechism and in the Westminster Confession of Faith.

7. For Mesopotamian law codes see James B. Pritchard, ed., *Ancient Near Eastern Texts Relating to the Old Testament* (Princeton: Princeton University Press, 1960), pp. 159-98.

8. Jospeh Fletcher, *Situation Ethics: The New Morality* (Philadelphia: Westminster, 1966).

9. For an extended discussion of the principle see Gerald A. Larue, *Old Testament Life and Literature* (Boston: Allyn & Bacon, 1968), p. 440.

10. Ibid., p. 31, f.n. 21.

11. On Friday, June 9, 1978, on the basis of a "revelation" given to Spencer W. Kimball, president of the Church of Jesus Christ of Latter-day Saints, after hours of prayer in the Upper Room of the Mormon Temple, it was announced that the Mormon Church would no longer bar Blacks from the Mormon priesthood. The basis for rejection rested upon passages found in the Mormon "Book of Moses," which was revealed to Joseph Smith in June 1830, and in the Mormon "Book of Abraham," which is supposed to be a translation of Egyptian manuscripts written by Abraham. Thus a new revelation replaces earlier ones.

12. See my article in *Free Inquiry* magazine titled "How the Old Testament Was Written," 7 (Winter, 1986/87): 30–37.

13. Larue, *Old Testament Life and Literature*, p. 175.

14. See Lord Raglan, *The Hero* (New York: Random House, 1959) and *Jesus in History and Myth,* ed. by R. Joseph Hoffmann and Gerald A. Larue (Buffalo, N.Y.: Prometheus, 1986).

15. Larue, *Old Testament Life and Literature*, p. 361.

16. For a discussion of biblical attitudes toward homosexuality, see Gerald A. Larue, *Homosexuality and the Bible* (a pamphlet) Amherst, N.Y.: American Humanist Association, 1983.

17. The female characteristics include compassion for children, weeping, etc., which are not considered to be masculine traits. For a reference to the god Atum, see Gerald A. Larue, *Ancient Myth and Modern Man* (New Jersey, 1975) p. 29.

2

Secular Humanism and the Bible

Theodor H. Gaster

Secular humanism's confrontation with the Bible, and hence with so-called "biblical ethics," rests on three main premises:

1. It contends that the canons of 'correct' human conduct should be projected out of man rather than injected into him—that is to say, they should issue out of man's perception and experience of his human situation rather than out of commandments enjoined by some superior and transcendental authority.

2. It rejects the idea that this supposedly external authority is a personal being rather than an abstract principle—that is to say, it rejects the notion of God, and hence that the Bible is His "word."

3. It regards some of the laws, institutions, and forms of behavior recorded in the Bible as below the moral standards developed in subsequent ages and as therefore unacceptable to current Western society.

All of these propositions, however, demand a second look, for closer scrutiny will reveal that they depend very largely on a series of confusions and misconceptions. The following observations are offered as a summary critique to this end. I should like, however, to make it clear at the outset that they are not motivated by any doctrinal bias or dogmatic preconceptions. The mantle of Elijah has not descended upon me; I stand (shivering to be sure) clad only in the scant (but, I hope, decent) loincloth woven during some sixty years of study and concern.

Theodor H. Gaster is professor emeritus of religion at Columbia University.

I.

The first crucial objection to secular humanism's position is that it tends to regard the meaning of the Bible as static—something fixed and immutable. The fact is, however, that the systems of religion founded on the Bible have always insisted that it is dynamic. Judaism maintains as a cardinal tenet that the written law (Torah) has always to be developed and amplified by the oral laws—that is, by the insights suggested by progressive study and by the experience of later ages. It enjoins such study as a continuous element of religion. There are, it says, seventy facets of the Torah, and it asserts in respect to conflicting views that "both these and those are words of the living God." Christian thinkers, for their part, have propounded the principle of *sensus plenior*—that is, that what is articulated in scripture in specific contexts transcends the particularity of such contexts and are simply paradigms and illustrations of universal "truths." "The light," as it says in the Book of Proverbs, "grows brighter and brighter until the day is at the full."

Back of this principle lies an apprehension of the fact that meaning is everywhere a junction between a writer's statement and his reader's experience and associations, and that it is therefore necessarily subjective and varied. Revelation is a two-way street; in other words, it is a process of collaboration between he who speaks and he who hears. The import and message of the scriptures thus entails variable interpretation, and religion, when founded on the Bible, depends as much on reading in as on reading out.

II.

We come next to secular humanism's rejection of the concept of God. In order to do justice to this concept it is necessary to understand the distinctive mind-set of the Ancient Near East, out of which the Bible issued.

The human stance of Ancient Near Eastern man was basically passive. Innocent of any serious knowledge of organic structures or of what we would recognize as "natural" laws, he attributed all activity in the world to outside agents. Human life thus consisted in being at every moment on the receiving end of these agents. A Babylonian would not say, for example, that he had a stomachache, but that a stomachache had him; and when a Hebrew prophet experienced ecstasy or had a sudden flash of insight, he said that the external 'spirit' had been breathed into or "inspired" him or that some external force touched him. The notion indeed survives in our own day, for we can describe the same condition either, in the active voice, as ecstasy—that is, as an active "standing outside" of one's normal senses, or passively as rapture—that is, a state of being seized. These external agents were seen as personal beings—gods or demons. Accordingly, all human acts and tempers were regarded as acts of these beings. This too survives in our own day, as when we speak of Fortune smiling on us, Time marching on, or of Disaster striking, and the like.

It is important to observe, however, that what was involved in the Ancient Near Eastern view was not in fact personification, as is commonly supposed. Personification means that some thing or phenomenon or abstract quality that one already knows otherwise is mentally and artificially transferred into the category of persons, as when a railroad engine is represented in a children's storybook as "Mr. Choo-choo." In the Ancient Near Eastern view, on the other hand, no such transference (or metaphor) took place; the external agents were seen as persons from the start. (It is, indeed, the failure to recognize this essential distinction that distorts our understanding.)

In back of this notion lay a view of the world as a conglomeration of disparate objects, phenomena, and beings—a multiverse. The religious expression of this was polytheism. (To use Latin terms, multiverse produces multideism.) There was, however, an alternative: the world, or a man's immediate environment, could be viewed holistically, as constituting a unified, systematic whole, a universe. In that case the innumerable gods would be coalesced into a single comprehensive god representing the overarching principle of the system, or cosmos. The religious expression of this is monotheism (or unideism). It was this holistic view that was held by the biblical writers and that became dominant in the 'official' religion of Israel, an additional reason for this being that Israel was historically a combination of several tribes whose different holistic gods had to be coalesced into a single deity controlling the entire federation: *e pluribus unum.*

What all this amounts to, then, is that when the Bible speaks of the acts and commandments of this monotheistic, transcendental god (Yahweh, Jehovah), it is speaking, *au fond,* of human situations. Thus, the God who brings the Israelites out of Egypt is basically an externalization, in personal terms, of their own human urge to get out, and when God comes down to Mount Sinai and Moses goes up, this is simply a graphic metaphor for the idea that any valid code of societal and individual conduct (a Torah) must be based on man's rising above his diurnal and mundane concerns and the overarching principles being reduced, for purposes of comprehension, to human levels.

In short, what secular humanists and most of the rest of us (including especially 'fundamentalists') have to get into our heads is that the best way of coming to grips with biblical ideology is to realize that the image of a personal god is simply a diagram, just as the symbol for triangle is not substantially a triangle, but merely the diagram of a geometrical entity and, just as in algebra, a + b = c represents an equation of quantities, but not of alphabetical characters. God, in other words, is an idol, in the exact (not popular) sense of the word (Greek, *eidulun,* 'image'). The Bible and all later Jewish thinking insist that he is noncorporeal, a verbal idol. An apprehension of this fact might seem, at first blush, to invalidate the cardinal Christian belief in the Incarnation. It should therefore be observed that, despite its reductive anthropo-morphic language, what this tenet really implies is not the transformation of a divine body onto a human body (Jesus), but the possession by a human body of the power to exemplify and reify the principle that we personify as God. Moreover, the incarnation of that principle in a human being is but one facet (persona) of a triune image that also includes its portrayal as a pervasive 'spirit' or genius.

Once this is realized, it becomes apparent that secular humanism's opposition to the concept of God is terminological rather than substantive, and is based, in the final analysis, on insensitivity to metpahor and poetry.

III.

This brings us squarely to secular humanism's refusal to recogize the Bible as the Word of God.

The point that has here to be made is that there is actually an appreciable difference between the Word of God and the Word from God, with which the latter is popularly confused. The concept of a word from God is simply a spin-off from the representation of God as a transcendental personal being who is then thought to have issued the Word as one of his operations. But if we see God as an abstract principle which *is* rather than a being which *does,* the Bible may be viewed as an integral part of his essence rather than as a product of an antecedent, distinct entity. The perceptions of the scriptural writers (fallible, to be sure because limited by man's imperfect equipment) are therefore instinct with what we personify as God (as, indeed, are all works of human genius), and it is in this sense that the Bible is a word of God. Jewish teaching in fact espouses the view in rabbinic dictim "the God of Israel, the Torah of Israel (in this context, the Old Testament as a whole) and the people of Israel (i.e., the collective historical experience) are basically one."

Two things especially make it possible to describe the Bible metaphorically as the Word of God.

First, the biblical writers see events in the perspective of a cosmic continuum, which they represent by theological imagery as the ongoing plan of a transcendental Person. This means that they possess an ultra-punctual, transtemporal significance that goes beyond the moments of their occurrence and is perpetually relevant. The Exodus of the Israelites from Egypt, for instance, exemplifies in a particular historical context the human urge of all men always to escape from every kind of bondage (including ignorance, obscurantism, and blatant materialism) and their readiness to trek through a figurative wilderness (even with lapses on the way) in order to reach a figurative Promised Land. So too, the destruction of the temple in Jerusalem is more than the loss of a piece of sacred real estate. The temple symbolizes the presence in human society of an awareness of that which God represents. The destruction of it thus pictoralized the eclipse of that awareness—a continuing alienation portrayed, in theological imagery, as the exile of God.

Second, the biblical writers see the laws and institutions of Israel as the social expression of the cosmic structure and design and therefore, in theological imagery, as the revealed dispensation of the personified Planner.

IV.

There is also another point that must be made in this connection. The Bible is not in itself religious: that term can be properly applied only to a human reaction to it. The Bible is literature, and literature involves not only the ideas of writers, but also art—that is, the technique of conveying ideas through the medium of words. Words, however—as a modern poet has put it—are shrunken garments; what is in a writer's mind and heart often outruns the limitations of language and vocabulary. The scriptural writers therefore eke out this shortcoming by resort to mythological representation. Thus the eventual elimination of error and evil—the enduring hope of mankind is represented by the prophet Isaiah as a future repetition of what is depicted in a Canaanite myth as the discomfiture of the primeval monster Leviathan at the beginning of the world. Similarly, the present imperfection of humanity is attributed to the misconduct of the first man and woman in a paradise abode, and the incarnation of the 'divine' essence in Jesus to a miraculous spiritual impregnation of a virgin—an idea that has parallels in other religious myths. In recent years, through the recovery of a good deal of Ancient Near Eastern literature by archaeological enterprise, we now have been able to recognize in the Bible many such mythological allusions previously missed. Unfortunately, in the traditional interpretation of scripture preached in church and synagogue such passages are still construed literally, so that a major part of orthodox religious belief becomes simply a tissue of myth. Modern theologians, it is true, have become increasingly aware of the need for what is termed 'deymthologization', but it is to be feared that they have tended to throw out the baby with the bath and to focus their attacks on the religious use of myth per se rather than on the acceptance of certain myths as religious dogmas. What we now need is not the abolition of myth in general, but rather the creation of new, contemporary mythic images and a deeper appreciation of the ideological idiom of the Bible. Indeed, if we could surmount our ingrained esthetic prejudices, we might even agree to portray God as a machine and not as a person—a lord or king!

V.

Last, there is the question of secular humanism's criticism of what it terms biblical ethics. The main objection that can be raised on this score is—as it seems to me—that there is here a basic confusion between morals and ethics. Morals are the standards traditionally recognized as necessary for ensuring what is deemed good in society and in individuals. These are determined by the exigencies of a particular society, and vary with its ever-changing culture. Ethics, on the other hand (on which, to be sure, morals are ultimately based), has as its province the determination of what constitutes 'good' in the first place and implies an antecedent premise. It is therefore possible to demur to particular forms of conduct implied in biblical narratives of prophesies or laws while leaving in abeyance the basic issue of the ethics that underlies them. We may decry, for instance, Jacob's behavior in wresting the birthright from Esau or the action of the Jews of Persia in making a holocaust of their non-Jewish neighbors in order to celebrate the failing of Haman's plot to make a holocaust of them. But we should not lose sight of two essential considerations: (a) By what criteria did Jacob justify his conduct as good or ethical? (b) Were such actions indeed regarded as acceptable, or do they but illustrate the fallibility of human beings in their judgment of ethical principles?

To answer these questions we must realize that the Ancient Near Eastern mind determined ethical criteria in its own distinctive manner, so it is a grave error of method to apply to them our own philosophical mind-set. The Old Testament principle is that the prime duty of men is to order his conduct in conformity with what is conceived as the proper system of the world, portrayed, in theological imagery, as the design of a transcendental Being. The main quality of this being—God— is defined in the Hebrew Bible as "Sedeq," which we conventionally render "righteousness." But this rendering is misleading: Sedeq—as the evidence of Semitic philology shows—is properly "that which is normal" or "proper." It is "right" in the sense of "What is the right way to Broadway?" or "What is the right way to cook a hamburger?" God is, not does, what is right in this sense. Human perception of it, however, is fallible, and the Bible describes these fallible perceptions. It describes attempts to reach the ideal, which is, indeed, the function of religion.

To sum up, secular humanism's attitude toward the Bible is open to the following criticisms:

1. It fails to penetrate the mind-set of the Ancient Near East, out of which the Bible issued.

2. It fails to realize that its objections are basically esthetic, not philosophical. It is really objecting to the ideological idiom of the biblical writers, which it takes literally.

3. It confuses theism with religion in general. Religion may be defunct as "the synthesis of thought, emotion, behavior, and symbolic ritual whereby, under traditional sanctions but with progressive insights, men attempt to determine and regulate their place in the scheme of things." It does not necessarily imply the concept of God as a substantive person, that is merely one form of religion. It is, however, distinct from philosophy in that it implies conduct and behavior and not mere speculation, and that it involves a posture of the entire self and not solely of the intellect.

Religion is as experience, not a doctrine. It is realized in specific moments. This point is beautifully illustrated in a passage of the Bible itself—a passage, I would add, which I have long regarded as the most profound in the entire Old Testament. It may be found in the Book of Exodus, where the confrontation of God and Moses on Mount Sinai is thus described:

> And the Lord came down in a cloud and stood with him there. Then the Lord passed before his [Moses'] face. And he [Moses] cried out: "the Lord, the Lord, a God compassionate and gracious," etc.

The Lord comes down. That is, what he represents is conveyed in reductive terms. *He comes down in a cloud.* That is, what he represents is apprehended only in a fuzz—through the mists of human perception. *He stood with him.* What he is is apprehended only in concrete situations, not in its doctrinal formulation. *He passed before:* what he represents is something not limited to a single place or moment, but it is a continuous, engaging process.

NOTE

1. This essay seeks to present in more literary form the substance of a paper offered in more conversational style at the *Free Inquiry* Conference in Richmond, Virginia, in October 1986.

3

Change and the Changeless[1]

John F. Priest

One of the most significant consequences of a literalistic/fundamentalist mode of biblical interpretation is that the contents of the Bible are flattened; they are seen as parts of an invisible whole. Since every part is inspired, indeed has God as its author, each possesses equal validity. The genealogical lists in 1 Chronicles and elsewhere, the magnificent call for justice by the prophet Amos, the incomprehensible imagery of the book of Revelation, and the Sermon on the Mount hold equal claim on the life of the believing reader. To be sure, most fundamentalists operate with a *de facto* canon within the canon;[2] but from a formal point of view, when pressed, there must be a reversion to the affirmation that the total canon is the authoritative, infallible, and inerrant word of God. To put it another way, the Bible, with God as its author, must mean the same thing to all people in all places at all times. Its validity and its authority are universal. In the midst of human change it remains changeless.

The purpose of this brief presentation is to draw attention to clear evidences of change and contradiction within the biblical material itself, and to extrapolate from that discussion some comments on the inter-relationship between biblical (religious) ethics and contemporary ethical issues, both religious and secular. I begin with an example that may seem trivial but is of import for the general thesis.

In one of the prophetic legends[3] concerning Eiljah, who flourished in the mid-ninth century B.C.E., God assigned the prophet three tasks, one of which was to designate a certain general Jehu to be king over

---

John F. Priest is chairman, Department of Religion, Florida State University.

Israel (1 Kings 19:16). This would entail overthrowing the existing dynasty. Elijah died, or disappeared (2 Kings 2:22), before he could fulfill that charge, and the responsibility passed to his successor, Elisha (2 Kings 9:1–4). He selected one of his prophetic associates to go to Jehu and announce that God had chosen him to be king. The gist of his message warrants citing. He proclaims that God has determined that Jehu "shall strike down the whole house of Ahab (the reigning dynasty) . . . for the whole house of Ahab shall perish; and I (God) will cut off from Ahab every male, bond or free, in Israel" (2 Kings 9:4–9, esp. v. 8).

Thus legitimated by the word and will of the God, Jehu carried out his destined role. He killed the Israelite king (Joram), and, for good measure, also the Judean king (Ahaziah) who happened to be visiting his fellow monarch. He then did away with the Queen Mother (Jezebel) and, to fulfill the divine command that the whole house should perish, he proceeded to wipe out seventy members of the royal house along with "his great men, and his familiar friends, until he left him none remaining" (2 Kings 9:17–10:11). Such bloody revolts are a commonplace of human history, in both antiquity and modernity. Yet we must note that this blood bath is said to be the direct consequence of the will of God.

About a century later another prophet, Hosea, delivered the following oracle (prophetic speech): "for yet a little while, and I will punish the house of Jehu for the blood of Jezreel (the site of the slaughter of Joram and Amaziah by Jehu), and I will put an end to the kingdom of the house of Israel. And on that day, I will break the bow of Israel in the valley of Jezreel" (Hosea 1:4–5). I shall defer comment on the moral issue involved in attributing to God approbation, even instigation, of Jehu's acts, though it should constitute a problem for one who assumes that the present text of the Bible contains the very words of God. My interest, rather, is in the change of attitude reflected in Hosea's stern criticism of those acts that earlier were attributed to a prophet, and through that prophet to God himself. The mass murders of Jehu, approved in the text of 2 Kings, now become the source of condemnation. This surely reflects change, historically conditioned, which calls into serious question the changelessness of the biblical text. Many, and much more serious examples of change of thought within the Bible itself could be adduced. I have selected this somewhat trivial episode simply to illustrate that realization of change is demanded by material internal to the Bible.

Let us now apply this principle of indubitable change to a biblical social issue. One of the oldest collections of laws in the Bible is found in Exodus 20:23–23:19, the so-called Covenant Code, or Book of the Covenant. While biblical scholars are not in total agreement, it seems most probable to date the essential content of this legal corpus to around 1000 B.C.E., give or take a century.[4] Several parts of the code deal with the institution of slavery. (I should add that enslavement of a fellow member of the covenant community is itself contrary to the egalitarian social system implicit in Israelite religion, but the economic facts of life prevailed in ancient Israel, as they do in modern America.) One of the provisions pertaining to slavery is an obvious effort to mitigate the odium of Hebrews having to endure bondage. The law states that "When you buy a Hebrew slave, he shall serve six years, and in the seventh he shall go out free for nothing" (Exod. 21:2). But a little later on in the code the following provision is found: "When a man sells his daughter as a slave, she shall not go out as the male slaves do" (Exod. 21:7). Male slaves are, in fact, indentured servants for six years; female slaves are slaves in perpetuity. (In fairness, it should be added that certain safeguards for the female slave are stated—e.g., 21:8–11; 21:20; 26–27—but the basic difference on automatic liberation for the male and not for the female is incontrovertible.)

One of the other major legal corpora in the Bible is the code of Deuteronomy (12:26). Scholarly opinions about the date and provenance of the Deuteronomic code remain much more diverse than is the case with the Covenant Code, but the following constitutes a generally representative position.[5] Deuteronomy, the legal section at least, is an amalgam of traditions from mainly northern circles of Levitical teachers who fled to the south after the fall of the northern kingdom in 721 B.C.E., and prophetic traditions current in both rural Israel and Judah. Though certainly containing much ancient material, the present form of the book dates from the middle of the seventh century B.C.E. Like the Covenant Code, Deuteronomy deals with the institution of slavery, and one basic difference is germane. The general provisions for dealing with the freed slave are much more generous in Deuteronomy than in Exodus, but the most striking change is the extension of liberation of the female slave: "If your brother, a Hebrew man, or a Hebrew woman, is sold to you, he shall serve you six years, and in the seventh year you shall let him go free" (Deut. 15:12). While efforts have been made to harmonize the two accounts, along with quite different provisions regarding slavery in yet another corpus, (Lev. 25:39–46)—e.g., release of the female slave is really implicit in Exodus, and Deuteronomy only makes explicit what is already implicit—the clearest reading of the text is that the authors of Deuteronomy have a more humanitarian view. Only the most tortuous exegesis can deny change, or at the very least, difference.[6]

I offer another possible instance of change between Exodus and Deuteronomy with some diffidence since exegesis of the passages remains complex and disputed.[7] The Decalogue, or Ten Commandments, is found in virtually the same form in Exodus 20:3–17 and Deuteronomy 5:7–21. (The so-called Ritual Decalogue in Exodus 34:14–26 is not in this instance germane.) The last commandment, according to most enumerations, deals with coveting. Most earlier scholars associated this with an inward attitude. Recent scholarship has tended to relate it to theft, and limit the earlier commandment, "Thou shalt not steal" (Exod. 21:15; Deut. 5:19), to kidnapping.[8] Adjudication between these two interpretations, is, in my judgment important, but not central to our present concern. I call attention to a minor but potentially significant change in the order of items coveted. The passage in Exodus reads: "You shall not covet your neighbor's house; you shall not covet your neighbor's wife, or his manservant, or his maidservant, or his ox, or his ass, or anything that is your neighbor's" (20:17). The Deuteronomic passage makes the following alteration: "Neither shall you covet your neighbor's wife; and you shall not desire your neighbor's house, his field, or his manservant, or his maidservant, his ox or his ass, or anything that is your neighbor's" (5:21). In another context it would be appropriate to deal with specific grammatical and lexical differences between the two passages,[9] but for our purposes I shall focus on one item only: the movement of wife to the primary position in the Deuteronomic version. Two different inferences may be drawn. First, it may be argued that there is really no difference between the two. The priority of "house" in the Exodus version means simply that "house" is all inclusive, and that the following references to wife, manservant, maidservant, and so on, are but examples of those things that pertain to a man's house, i.e., his property. Listing of the wife as the first item of his property indicates the priority of her importance, but still as property.

Second, however, one could conclude that the authors of Deuteronomy desire to indicate the absolute prior value and importance of the wife and thus set her apart from all other property pertaining to the man. If the latter interpretation is adopted, we may infer that there was a change that shifted women from the list of chattel goods—

like property, slaves, and animals—and addressed her on the level of full humanity. I am persuaded by this interpretation, though I admit that here I may be guilty of reading into the text the process of exegesis that I so deplore in others. In any case, our examples of Hosea's changed interpretation of the role of God and the prophet in the slaughter perpetuated by Jehu, and the obvious extension of slave liberation to women in Deuteronomy, compared with the legislation in Exodus, clearly indicates that change does appear in different biblical texts.

These examples could be almost infinitely multiplied, but they are sufficient at this juncture. Fundamentalist interpretation is at least consistent on one point. If any change be permitted, then all change is possible. The line must be held from Genesis to Revelation. Withdrawal at *any* point is potential capitulation at *every* point. This is known as the slippery slide argument.[10] You give up a little thing here, and another little thing there, and finally you throw the whole book away.

This apparent strength of consistency is, of course, a fatal flaw to any objective viewer—even a subjective objective viewer. There is change, openly declared change, in a text claimed to be changeless. In addition to change, we need to mention internal contradiction. By contradiction I am not referring to simple discrepancies in chronologies, geographical locales, or numbers of men under arms in a particular conflict, though again these would, or should, cause embarrassment for thoroughgoing inerrantists. Rather, I refer to specific moral or ethical injunctions that are not only at variance but in direct opposition. I shall mention only two, the first being somewhat trivial, the second of considerable contemporary consequence.

In two successive verses in Proverbs we read: "Answer not a fool according to his folly, lest you be like him yourself. Answer a fool according to his folly, lest he become wise in his own eyes" (26:4–5). Anyone who has made the barest beginning into the study of sapiential literature readily understands this apparent contradiction. The sages of the ancient Near East, and elsewhere, were pragmatic. They were, to use that horrendous word, contextual. In some circumstances you recognize that to reason with a fool only confirms him in his own foolishness. Thus, you refrain from argumentation. On other occasions, it appears that the fool can be taught. Then you do enter into debate in the hope that he may see the error of his ways. There is, therefore, no significant exegetical problem except for those who read the Bible in a totally noncontextual or ahistorical manner, where each sentence, indeed each word, is imbued with divine authority obligatory on all people, in all places, and at all times. These two verses simply will not fit into that hermeneutical context. You cannot be divinely commanded "to answer not" and "to answer." If you choose between the two, then human reason is operative, not the divine word.

My second example is of more substance and importance since it has entered into the contemporary political scene through the exegetical expertise of our president. There was a prophetic oracle prized enough in the tradition to be included in two collections. There are minor textual differences, but the gist of the oracle remains constant. The crucial common phrases are: "They shall beat their swords into ploughshares and their spears into pruning hooks, nation shall not lift up sword against nation, neither shall they learn war anymore" (Isa. 2:4 and Mic. 4:3). The import is clear. Human propensity for war is to be transmuted into the pursuit and achievement of peace. In another prophetic collection, however, we read: "Proclaim this among the nations. Make holy the act of war. Stir up the mighty men. Let all men of war draw near. Let them come up. Beat your ploughshares into swords and your pruning hooks into spears. Let the weak say, 'I am a warrior'" (Joel 3:9–10). The exegete who employs the historical method can make sense out of the apparent discrepancy between these two passages. I take the passages in Isaiah and Micah as simply different recensions of the same oracle. Both passages, in Isaiah and Micah on the one hand and Joel on the other, are set in an eschatological context. That is, both are speaking of that momentous time when the reign of the god of Israel will become actual in the lives of the nations. There is agreement on the certainty of that trial, but there was disagreement on the details that would accompany the advent of that trial. One view, expressed in the Isaiah-Micah oracle, dreamed of a reign that emerged through and was consummated in peace and harmony among all peoples. The other, expressed in Joel, anticipated the cataclysmic conflict that must precede.

It is possible that the viewpoint expressed in Joel allowed for establishment of an ultimate reign of peace (Joel 3:18–21 makes that conclusion problematical), but our concern is with the consequence of a flat ahistorical reading of the texts, which are clearly contradictory from that perspective. Either peace or war may be commanded, but not both.

I have intentionally ignored a commonly cited instance of both change and contradiction; the movement from the Old Testament to the New. In a number of passages in the New Testament, most trenchantly in the so-called Sermon on the Mount (Matt. 5–7, with some parallels in Luke 6:20–49), "You have heard it said . . . but I say . . ." the implication is made, or at least the inference can be drawn, that the new age inaugurated by Jesus has set aside the laws given to Israel. I have ignored this approach for two reasons. On the one hand it leads to an unnecessary and invidious division between the two biblical communities. On the other, the New Testament writers equivocate. For some the New Age totally supersedes the Old; for some the New Age sets aside some aspects, mainly ceremonial rites, of the Old but retains other aspects; for there is direct and unbroken continuity between Old and New. I cannot explore, in this context, the difficult problem of the historical and, especially, the theological relationships between Israel and the church, but that some interpreters do drive a wedge between the authority of the teachings of the two communities is of profound consequence for those who maintain that the entire Bible is the direct and immutable Word of God, binding upon all people, in all places, and at all times. Historical study may help us understand the nuances of change and of continuity between the two communities and their respective scriptures.[11]

Fundamentalist interpretation, in the last analysis, must eschew the historical for the timeless. Thus, bizarre exegetical methods (principally typology and allegory)[12] are required to explain, or explain away, conflicting injunctions found in the two Testaments. This is not innately different from the attempts to reconcile contradictions within each Testament itself, but it assumes a new dimension in that the absolute authority of the Old Testament as the word(s) of God must somehow be brought into line with the Christian assertion that Jesus is unique and supreme. Exploration of that issue, however, is more suited to a setting which is primarily concerned with theological matters.

What then of the Bible with respect to contemporary social and ethical issues?[13] Space does not permit detailed discussion of specific issues. What follows is intended to be simply paradigmatic. The negation of the assertion that the Bible must mean the same thing to all people, in all places, and at all times, does not carry with it the correlative assertion that the Bible *may* not mean anything to anybody outside the specific historical setting in which the documents that became the Bible emerged. It is one thing, and a necessary one, to recognize the historically conditioned nature of the biblical materials. That was the central point of the illustrations adduced to demonstrate change and contradiction internal to the Bible. Such a recognition does not permit us simply to address a contemporary social question on the basis of timeless biblical authority.

For example, it is indisputable that the Bible (in parts of it at least) sanctions slavery, capital punishment, war, and the derogation of women. It is likewise indisputable that biblical texts condemning homosexuality and (probably) sexual activity outside the prescribed marital limits are to be found. A fundamentalist approach to scripture finds in biblical texts the last word of authority: "The Bible says. . .". Many secular humanists, not all I am happy to say, regard the Bible as an antiquated document that has no counsel or guidance to the contemporary scene. I propose that the careful historical study of the Bible can correct, or at least modify, both erroneous positions.

Historical study can assist us in understanding the conditions under which the biblical material emerged and to become aware of significant changes to be found in that material. What did it mean in its context? Those of us for whom the Bible continues to have considerable significance, go on to ask the question, "Is it true?" We don't mean: Is it factual? Did the fish actually swallow Jonah? Did the sun stand still in answer to the prayer of Joshua? Our question, rather, is this: "Does this text contain a truth that transcends its original historical context? Does it say something that is of continuing validity for the human condition? Our historical study can sometimes provide a clue to the answering of such questions.

On the one hand, such study may make it quite clear that a particular teaching is so time conditioned that it may and must be relegated to an interesting but now irrelevant chapter of ancient history. At other times such study may point to the significant contribution that some biblical material may make to our continuous pursuit for meaning and order in human society.

The Bible is certainly to be interpreted in terms of change, even in terms of contradiction. But if there is anything changeless in our world, that also may be found in the biblical material. Our task is to discern between what is subject to change and what is changeless. Historical study of the biblical material itself points us toward a fruitful hermeneutical stance.[14]

NOTES

1. Two prefatory comments are in order. First, the text of this article has been only slightly changed from the original form which was intended for oral presentation. Second, since the article is designed for the general reader bibliographical references have, for the most part been limited to reference works which are readily accessible

and nontechnical in nature. More detailed studies may be found in the bibliographies appended to the works cited.

2. Canon within canon simply means that certain groups apply more importance to certain parts of the Bible, in practice, while formally assigning equal validity to the entire canon.

3. Legend, as here used, refers to a story about a folk hero. The question of the historicity or nonhistoricity of the story is bracketed.

4. See, e.g., *Interpreter's Dictionary of the Bible,* (hereafter *IDB*) iii, 82f. *Interpreter's Bible,* i, 843f. Noth, *Exodus* (Philadelphia: 1962), 175.

5. See *IDB* i, 831–838. This article is by G. von Rad, a scholar who has had the most impact on studies in Deuteronomy in this generation. It is fair to say, however, that his views are currently being subjected to considerable revision. See *IDB,* 229–232.

6. Although both examples of growing "humanitarianism" cited above do represent chronological development, I do not mean to imply a kind of inevitable evolutionary improvement. Biblical attitudes did change, but there was regression as well as progress. Even to use those terms lays the interpreter open to a subjective perspective.

7. A good nontechnical introduction to the Ten Commandments as a whole is given by Walter J. Harrelson, *IDB* iv, 569–573. (Harrelson has also written a stimulating book relating the Decalogue to the contemporary scene, *The Ten Commandments and Human Rights* (Philadelphia: 1980). For a superb technical treatment of the Decalogue, see Brevard Childs, *Exodus* (Philadelphia: 1974) 384–439. A full bibliography of both ancient and modern works may be found there.

8. See J. J. Stamm and M. E. Andrew, *The Ten Commandments in Modern Research* (London: 1962) esp. 101–107; Childs, *Exodus,* 425–428.

9. The issues here are highly technical in nature. They include matters of word order, shift of verbs between Exodus and Deuteronomy, punctuation, and variants to be found in the early Greek and Samaritan versions. Scholars are widely divided as to whether the commandment deals only with attitude, only with act, or with both attitude and act. They differ also as to whether the shift of wife in Deuteronomy from house in Exodus as the first item in the list indicates any genuine change in the status of women. Thus, the interpretation adopted in the text must be viewed with some reserve, though I am convinced of it.

10. See Stephen T. Davis, *The Debate About the Bible* (Philadelphia: 1977) esp. 83–93.

11. The literature on the relationships between the Testaments, always a matter of primary concern for Christian theology, has assumed a new dimension in light of renewed efforts at Jewish-Christian dialogue. I regret to note that with rare exceptions Christians from the first century C.E. to the present, however much they claim to value the "Old" Testament have claimed that in some manner the Hebrew scriptures have been superseded.

12. Typology asserts that certain persons, events or institutions in the Old Testament are models of corresponding realities in the New Testament. Their full meaning is not understood until their later reappearance in the life of Jesus, the Church or Christian faith. Allegory is even more fanciful, assuming that a story may have a surface meaning but that it also and more importantly has a spiritual

meaning. Thus, in the parable of the Good Samaritan, the wounded man is fallen humanity, the Good Samaritan is Jesus, the inn is the church, and so on. One uses allegory to support positions arrived at on other grounds and with no genuine rootage in the text being interpreted.

13. An excellent discussion may be found in Bruce C. Birch and Larry Rasmussen, *Bible and Ethics in the Christian Life* (Minneapolis: 1976). An excellent treatment, limited to a study of Paul, which makes full use of the historical method is Victor P. Furnish's *The Moral Teaching of Paul* (Nashville: 1979).

14. One of the most balanced treatments is that of Paul Achtemeier, *The Inspiration of Scripture* (Philadelphia: 1980). I deal with the matter briefly in *Free Inquiry* 2:2, 15–19.

4

The Bible and Anti-Semitism

Frank E. Eakin, Jr.

INTRODUCTION

It is an unfortunate but undisputed fact that ecclesiastically oriented anti-Semitism emerged early in the life of the church. It is impossible now to determine whether a preconceived and pervasive anti-Semitism influenced the thought perspective of the New Testament materials as they were written or whether these materials, once formulated, were victimized by a latent but emerging anti-Semitic Christendom to encourage the maturation of a fully developed anti-Semitism in the church. What is clear is that anti-Semitism did exist from an early time on and that some of the New Testament writings were generally interpreted to encourage such a pattern of thought rather than serving to abate its vitriolic venom of prejudice and hatred. Thus, we debate not the fact of the disease but rather the causes bringing about the phenomenon and perhaps over what should be labeled an anti-Semitic act.

Popular use has so distorted "anti-Semitism" that a dictionary definition describes the person who espouses this view as "one who is hostile to or discriminates against Jews."[1] The more appropriate designation, obviously, is anti-Judaism. This phenomenon has a long history, and as some Christian apologists are quick to note, it began before the Christian era. Unfortunately, it was redefined and intensified with the emergence of Christianity. Thus, while conceding to common use with the words "anti-Semite" and "anti-Semitism," we should recognize the specificity of this enacted prejudice, anti-Judaism.[2]

Frank E. Eakin, Jr., is Camp-Cousins Professor of Religion, University of Richmond.

THEOLOGICAL ANTI-SEMITISM

It is undisputed that anti-Semitism existed prior to the emergence of the Christian church. Its indications can be found even in the Hebrew scriptures: for example, in the events surrounding the exodus of one end of the chronological spectrum and in the story of Esther on the other end. What emerges new with the church is *theological* anti-Semitism, a new genre of the hideous phenomenon. According to this perception it was not only permissible but mandated that Christians seek to rectify that great wrong done to Jesus of Nazareth. Deriving from this understanding plus an evolving Christology, the concept of deicide arose by the second Christian century. Circumstances mandated that the conflict between Judaism and Christianity would be particularly vitriolic. As noted by Rosemary Ruether:

> The sad truth of religious history is that one finds that special virulence, which translates itself into diabolizing and damnation, only between groups which pose rival claims to exclusive truth within the same religious symbol system.[3]

Christianity's affirmation that Jesus was the Christ, i.e., the Messiah, was faith's reaction to the traumatic cross-resurrection event on the part of Jesus' closest followers. This affirmation was joined to altered perceptions of God, man, and the world when compared with traditional Judaism once the church entered significantly into and was sharply influenced by its Hellenistic environment. Both this affirmation and these differing perceptions served to ignite anti-Semitism. Christian writings, later to be accorded the status of scripture, recounted Jesus' condemnation of the Jews to whom much had been entrusted and little returned; recalled the Jews' obduracy in responding to Jesus' call to commitment, and affirmed the Jews' ultimate responsibility for the death of Jesus. All of these factors conjoined to stimulate anti-Semitism, most especially once the Christians gained sufficient political strength for injecting them.

Such prejudice was not limited to the early centuries of the church's growth and development, nor even to the Middle Ages with the constant recurrences of virulent anti-Semitism. Numerous more contemporary statements of anti-Semitism are also available, for we within Christendom have demonstrated ourselves to be amazingly nondiscriminating as regards those elements of the past that should be preserved. One such statement of anti-Semitism is found in James Daane's 1965 publication entitled *The Anatomy of Anti-Semitism and Other Essays on Religion and Race:*

> According to the New Testament records, Jews desired, plotted and promoted the execution of Jesus (Matthew 27:1). No rewriting of history by those interested in freeing the Jews from responsibility for the crucifixion, or by script writers of modern movies, dispels these claims of the New Testament historical records . . . . All this is not a fabric of prejudice against the Jews but the claims of the historical record of the New Testament.[4]

An obvious problem associated with the position suggested by Daane and others is the loose way the word "historical" is attached to the Gospel writings. From a Jewish perspective it has long been recognized that a significant portion of the New Testament writings, especially the Gospels, constitute a type of midrashic or homiletical commentary directed to the community that developed following the death and affirmed resurrection of Jesus.[5] Certainly such homiletical material is not the type to which we usually apply the adjective "historical." Nor is the literary genre, Gospel, a biographical statement but a unique form that attempts to express the truth of God's act among men. Consciously, it is not biographical. This does not mean that it is either anti-historical or ahistorical; rather, it simply acknowledges that the mere recording of historical data was not the purpose of the Gospel writers. The focus was upon *Geschichte,* the significance of the events, rather than upon *Historie,* the verifiable facts of history.[6]

Viewing the New Testament in this midrashic sense opens new avenues of interpretation. Once we expurgate the view that limits us to interpreting the New Testament only as literal, historical record, it may be set more squarely in its historical and theological context and the material may speak freely from within in an unmuzzled fashion rather than having imposed upon it subjective perceptions. In short, we are freed to do exegesis rather than to engage in eisegesis.

Any student of the New Testament recognizes the fallacy of basing anti-Semitism upon New Testament texts. Nonetheless, history records all too clearly that significant problems have emerged as a result of noncritical reading of the New Testament texts, using eisegesis rather than exegesis. It would be relatively simple to prove a church/synagogue antagonism, an anti-Jew bias, or a law/grace antipathy by interpreting the material uncritically.

As painful as the reckoning may be for Christians, Arthur Roy Eckhardt expressed most clearly what others have also suggested, that "antisemitism is . . . the war of Christians against Jesus the Jew."[7] Ethically, the intent of the Gospels is usually read to mean that the demand of Jesus' teaching upon the believer is all-encompassing, requiring a discipleship of absolute commitment, even to the point of following Jesus to the result of his own mission. This involves an unappealing ego-renunciation. One way of dealing with this discomfort is to react negatively to those who are scripturally identified with Jesus' rejection—the Jews. Thus, at least partially, anti-Semitism is the attempt by Christians to rid themselves of that part of Jesus' mission which is most offensive, namely, the suffering servant's role. The irony, of course, is that this role is explicable only within a Jewish context. The reaction to the Jew, then, is a blow against both the death of Jesus and the Christian commission to assume a vocation parallel to his. It is a harsh solution, but surely Eckardt is correct when he asserts that, should the choice be either to preserve anti-Semitism and maintain the church or abolish the church if this be the necessary prerequisite for eliminating anti-Semitism, then the church must go![8]

THE PAULINE PREPARATION

Indicative of the early reaction of Christianity to Judaism, attention is turned now to two Pauline writings, which have helped to undergird Christian anti-Semitism: Romans 9–11 and the Galatian correspondence. Clearly, it is impossible to develop these materials definitively, but it is important to recognize their negative potential, whether or not it was so intended by the writer.

To say that Paul's writings are frequently engimatic is understatement, but because of that fact Paul's attitude toward Judiasm will continue to be debated. One cannot ignore his personal relationship to Pharisaism (Phil. 3:5) and a concern for fellow-Jews that expressed itself consistently as he went first to the Jewish community in each city he visited. Nonetheless, some of the ideas found in Paul's letters have formed an essential foundation for Christian anti-Semitism, most especially that of God's rejection of the Jews.

Friedrich Heer is a good example of one who decries Paul's contribution to the problems of anti-Semitism. He argues that it was Paul who denied Judaism its continuing messianic heritage and served as the spiritual mentor for St. Augustine, who completed "the process of turning the 'true church' into a religion of celibates. . . ."[9] Emphasizing the impact of Paul, he states:

> Jewish festivities retain to this day this note of joy. Early Christian love-feasts basked in a similar joy. Christianity after St. Paul denounced the fleshly, earthbound hope of the Jews and branded the Jews as lascivious, fleshly and sexually obsessed—right up to the trails of the Third Reich.[10]

Romans 9–11 is one passage often cited as a foundation for anti-Semitism.[11] This is one of the clearest Paulist statements regarding the role of the Jews in the divine *Heilsgeschichte*. Paul had an abiding concern for the salvation of the Jew (10:1), but at the same time he was convinced that faith was the only way of effecting the proper relationship between God and man (10:5–11). Because faith is the essential ingredient, he could affirm that "there is no distinction between Jew and Greek . . ." (10:12). Did this mean, therefore, that any special role for the Jew was rejected? Not according to Paul's ultimate conclusion, for he argued that Jewish obduracy to the Christian proclamation was divinely implanted. It was only because the Jews refused to hear the Gospel that the message was delivered to the Gentiles (11:25). Has God thus rejected Israel? Not according to Paul. The eventual Jewish reaction will be one of acceptance of the Christ, and thus the Jew along with the Gentile will be saved (11:26–32). Rosemary Ruether, however, has suggested that Paul did not mean this to apply indiscriminately to all of Judaism. She notes that Paul was authentically referring to a "converison of the Jews":

> This "mystery" in Paul does not suggest in any way an ongoing validity of the Mosaic covenant as a community of salvation in its own right. Contemporary ecumenists who use Romans 11 to argue that Paul does not believe that God has rejected the people of the Mosaic covenant speak out of good intentions, but inaccurate exegesis. For Paul, there is, and has always been, only one true covenant of salvation. This is the covenant of the promise, given *apart from the Law,* to Abraham and now manifest in those who believe in Abraham's spiritual son, Christ. The people of the Mosaic covenant do not now and never have had any way of salvation through the Torah itself. God never intended to save his people through the Law.[12]

This quotation raises an issue addressed also in the Galatian correspondence, namely, does Judaism *per se* have a continuing rationale for being. The majority of expositors would wish to respond affirmatively. To the contrary, Gregory Baum in the Introduction to Ruether's *Faith and Fratricide* and addressing specifically Romans 9–11, states:

> All attempts of Christian theologians to derive a more positive conclusion from Paul's teaching in Romans 9–11 (and I have done this as much as others) are grounded in wishful thinking. What Paul and the entire Christian tradition taught is unmistakably negative: the religion of Israel is now superseded, the Torah abrogated, the promises fulfilled in the Christian Church, the Jews struck with blindness, and whatever remains of the election of Israel rests as a burden upon them in the present age.[13]

Will Herberg emphasized the centrality of the covenant for biblical thought,[14] but, contrary to Ruether, he did not envision the Christian covenant to supplant the Israelite covenant. He stated that "Christian faith thus brings into being and defines a new convenant, which is new not in the sense of supplanting the old but in the sense of extending and enlarging it. . . ."[15] C. H. Dodd, writing about Romans 9–11, noted that the issue of Israel's rejection presented a serious difficulty "to all who accepted the historic revelation in the Hebrew Scriptures as the starting-point of Christianity (as Paul did, and all Christians at the time, so far as we know). . . ."[16] Thus, on the one hand, Herberg's emphasis would be on covenant extension rather than supersession, while on the other hand, Dodd addresses the paradox of Christianity being rooted in Judaism but unable to deal with Judaism's rejection of Jesus.

Rosemary Ruether will not let the interpreter move so adroitly around the problems. She emphasizes that Paul envisioned two distinct eons, suggesting that the "Mosaic and the Christian covenants have no common inheritance."[17] There are two eons represented by Abraham's two wives in Paul's Galatian correspondence (4:21–31). Sarah represents the eon of freedom found in the Christ, and Hagar that of slavery characteristic of the Mosaic covenant. The real issue, therefore, is whether Israel had completed its *raison d'être* when it gave birth to the Christ. This would be a complete rejection of the *Heilsgeschichte* concept, whose interpretation is difficult to accept as the Pauline position. Since the data is open to either interpretation—namely, ongoing continuity or total breach —most indicators would align Paul with a sense of continuity existent between the historic faith of Judaism and the faithful community finding expression in Jesus as the Christ. While personal preference would be given to this interpretation, it is the total breach or absolute supplanter view that stands behind anti-Semitism. Ruether's judgment is absolutely correct, given her interpretation that "Paul's position was unquestionably that of anti-Judaism."[18] Reading Paul in terms of two eons—that of Christian faith supplanting the Jewish faith, or God having rejected Judaism—all such hermeneutical orientations serve to encourage, indeed to foster, anti-Semitism within the Christian community.

MEDIEVAL ICONOGRAPHY

To make concrete what can appear overly hypothetical, examples of the manner by which the anti-Semitism of the church was "canonized" in the iconography of several medieval French cathedrals can serve our purpose. According to Henry Kraus, "As the tide of anti-Semitism swept through Western Europe during the twelfth and thirteenth centuries, it was reflected in all media of religious art and liturgy."[19] Thus, the impact of the church's anti-Semitic spirit might be approached from numerous perspectives. Regardless, the result is clear. The venom of anti-Semitism associated with "official" or "establishmment" Christianity—the anti-Semitism of medieval Biblical interpretation—was transmitted and focused in the "popular" Christianity of the masses. Whereas I have done only preliminary investigation into this phenomenon, I shall note three examples of this "canonization" process, all of which are obviously grounded in biblical understandings:

(1) At the Strasbourg Cathedral's south porch, which is a thirteenth-century structure, there is a larger-than-life piece of statuary that portrays the synagogue, i.e., Judaism, as a beautiful but blinded woman. This depiction, which is found at numerous sites and in both stone and stained-glass iconography, portrays the inability of the Jew to recognize and thus to accept truth.[20] Quite frequently such depictions portray the Jewess holding a broken staff, i.e., no longer viable or usable.

(2) At the thirteenth-century Chartres Cathedral, a particularly telling depiction has a series of five lancet windows located beneath the south rose window. One of the lancet windows portrays the Virgin Mary, the central focus of the Chartres Cathedral, while the remaining four lancet windows portray the four evangelists seated atop the shoulders of the four prophets: Isaiah, Daniel, Ezekiel, and Jeremiah.[21] One interpretation of this iconographic representation suggests the theme

of Christianity's supersession of Judaism. Another possible interpretation indicates that the reduced size of the four evangelists "symbolizes their dependency upon the teachings of the Old Testament."[22] Clearly the latter interpretation depicts a more realistic assessment of Christianity's relationship to and dependency upon Judaism for its self-perception. It is unfortunate that historically the former view has dominated and has fed anti-Semitism.

(3) Very early on, the promise-fulfillment motif became part of this supersession theme. At the twelfth-century Church of La Madeleine, located at Vezelay, St. Paul is depicted on a capital relief within the nave "grinding out the grain of the Old Testament in Christianity's 'mystic mill,'" the grain brought to it by the Hebrew prophets.[23] Such a depiction indicates the true reason for the Hebrew scriptures: to give prophecies of Jesus as the Christ. Again, the Jewish scriptures are essentially valueless unless their relationship to Christianity is established, a relationship that can be clarified only by one such as Paul standing within the Christian tradition.

These iconographic representations firmly planted the anti-Semitism of the medieval era. As expressed by one writer, the purpose of these forms—and he was talking specifically about conversion art—was to prove "the superiority of the Christian faith; this art reflected the continuing polemic which all through the Middle Ages Christian thinkers felt called on to conduct with Judaism and the Jews."[24]

CONCLUSION

Rosemary Ruether has correctly indicated that "Christianity confronted Judaism with a demand for a conversionist relationship to its own past that abrogated that past, in the sense that that past itself no longer provided a covenant of salvation."[25] Such an either-or stance, however, was characteristic of the period of the church rather than the period of Jesus. There is not sufficient evidence to assign such an attitude to Jesus of Nazareth. While one cannot suggest the exact nature of the phenomenon, it seems entirely possible that some type of Jewish-Christian body might have survived even into the present had not a battle for supremacy and control of the symbol structure erupted between the followers of Jesus and those Jews who could not affirm Jesus to be the Messiah. Regardless, the conflict associated with Christianity's singular force, its adamant insistence upon control of the faith symbol system, and its Hellenization combined to bring about Christianity's almost total breach with Judaism.

The question for the future, however, is whether that breach is irreparable, not for the purpose of assimilation but for meaningful association. It is probably fair to answer that query in the affirmative, so long as the majority of Christians refuse to evaluate seriously their own roots within Judaism as well as Christianity's place as a universal religion among world religions. Essentially, the issues are twofold. On the one hand, central to the debate is the issue of authority, most especially that of biblical authority. On the other hand, it is also a fact that so long as a majority of Christians affirm that Judaism is not a viable vehicle for one's relationship with God and man, that in essence one must become Christian to achieve that status, then it is inevitable that anti-Semitism will continue. It will continue either by virtue of misguided but well-intentioned activity that may be labeled passively or covertly anti-Semitic, or it will continue because of overt attempts to coerce the conversion of the Jew, regardless of how subtle those attempts may be.

NOTES

1. *Webster's Seventh New Collegiate Dictionary* (Springfield, Mass.: G. & C. Merriam Company, Publishers, 1967), p. 40.

2. See Hannah Arendt, *Antisemitism* [Part One of *The Origins of Totalitarianism*] (New York: Harcourt, Brace & World, Inc., 1968), pp. vii-xii, where she comments helpfully on the distinction between "Religious Jew-hatred" and anti-Semitism.

3. Rosemary Ruether, *Faith and Fratricide: The Theological Roots of Anti-Semitism* (New York: The Seabury Press, 1974), p. 30.

4. James Daane, *The Anatomy of Anti-Semitism and other Essays on Religion and Race* (Grand Rapids, Mich.: William B. Eerdmans Publishing Company, 1965), p. 21. See also numerous other places in the tract for similar statements.

5. I have addressed this in Frank E. Eakin, Jr., *We Believe in One God: Creed and Scripture* (Bristol, Ind.: Wyndham Hall Press, 1985), pp. 119-120.

6. See "Historie," in Van A. Harvey, *A Handbook of Theological Terms* (New York: The Macmillan Company, 1964), p. 121.

7. Arthur Roy Eckardt, *Elder and Younger Brothers* (New York: Charles Scribner's Sons, 1967), p. 22, developed pp. 22-30. See also by the same author *Christianity and the Children of Israel* (New York: King's Crown Press, 1948), in which a clear statement against anti-Semitism is expressed from a neo-Orthodox perspective.

8. Eckardt, *Christianity and the Children of Israel,* pp. 97-98, 177.

9. Friedrich Heer, *Gods's First Love: Christians and Jews Over Two Thousand Years,* trans. Geoffrey Skelton (New York: Weybright and Talley, 1970), p. 30.

10. Heer, *God's First Love: Christians and Jews over Two Thousand Years,* pp. 30–31.

11. See Gregory Baum, *Is the New Testament Anti-Semitic?* rev. ed. (Glen Rock, N.J.: Paulist Press, 1965), pp. 275–348. A volume such as *The Jewish Question,* by Arno Clemens Gaebelein (New York: Publication Office "Our Hope," 1912), is characteristic of a "soft" anti-Semitism. Gaebelein assumes that it is necessary for Israel yet to be saved, implicitly asserting thereby the ineffectiveness of the Jewish faith. See also Douglas R. A. Hare, *The Theme of Jewish Persecution of Christians in the Gospel According to St. Matthew* (Cambridge: The University Press, 1967), pp. 149ff.

12. Ruether, *Faith and Fratricide,* p. 106.

13. Gregory Baum in *Faith and Fratricide,* p. 6.

14. Will Herberg, *Faith Enacted as History,* ed. with an Introduction by Bernhard W. Anderson (Philadelphia: The Westminster Press, 1976), p. 48.

15. Herberg, *Faith Enacted as History,* p. 50. While beginning from radically different presuppositions, see also Walther Eichrodt, *Theology of the Old Testament,* I–II, trans. J. A. Baker (Philadelphia: The Westminster Press, 1961, 1967) for the best exposition of the centrality of the covenant in biblical faith.

16. C. H. Dodd, *The Epistle of Paul to the Romans* in *The Moffatt New Testament Commentary,* ed. James Moffatt (London: Hodder and Stoughton, Limited, 1932), p. 150.

17. Ruether, *Faith and Fratricide,* p. 103.

18. Ruether, *Faith and Fratricide,* p. 104.

19. Henry Krause, *The Living Theatre of Medieval Art* (Bloomington: Indiana University Press), p. 149.

20. See Kraus, *The Living Theatre of Medieval Art,* pp. 139–162 for a good discussion of "Anti-Semitism in Medieval Art."

21. See Painton Cowen, *Rose Windows* (San Francisco: Chronicle Books/ A Prism Edition, 1979), pp. 14–15.

22. Lawrence Lee, George Seddon, Francis Stephens, *Stained Glass* (New York: Crown Publishers, Inc., 1976), pp. 77.

23. Kraus, *The Living Theatre of Medieval Art,* p. 145.

24. Kraus, *The Living Theatre of Medieval Art,* p. 159.

25. Ruether, *Faith and Fratricide,* p. 80.

5

The Moral Rhetoric of the Gospels

R. Joseph Hoffmann

One of the services performed by the evangelical movement in its latest recrudescence is to remind us that Christianity is not chiefly about ethics. To call this a service may seem odd, given the assumption—one shared by most nonfundamentalists and humanists alike—that if Christianity has anything to contribute to contemporary culture it must be in the area of heightening the moral consciousness of the human family. Thus when the Catholic bishops speak out against the arms race, or the World Council of Churches (WCC) decries world hunger—problems against which it is very easy to speak out—one is led to believe that the church is here exercising that high moral vision of which Jesus of Nazareth was the perfect embodiment. Were Jesus to return today, the thinking goes, he would endorse the bishops' letter and side with the WCC against poverty. He would be against apartheid because moral people are. He would support liberation struggles everywhere because he would believe in the principles of self-determination and democracy. He would not quite be a communist, as moral people believe in God and make money to endow those institutions that propagate Christian teaching; but he would not approve of the more crass forms of free enterprise since these, like poverty, have dehumanizing effects. One has no trouble imagining the Jesus of a secularized Christian church approving birth control, if not unequivocally abortion on demand; loving relationships between unmarried persons or persons of the same sex; or, indeed, the entire social agenda of the Riverside Church. True enough, this Jesus of the

R. Joseph Hoffmann is senior lecturer in the Division of Religious Studies, LaTrobe University, Australia.

pop-theologians is looking a bit addlepated these days, and his chief advertisers—the Reverend William Sloane Coffin, Professor Harvey Cox, and the now-antiquated Death of God movement of the late sixties— are quietly atoning for their abuse of biblical scholarship. But the Jesus of the social gospel, whether of Gustavo Gutierrez or James Hal Cone or Rosemary Ruether, is a perdurable character in the life of the con- temporary church. Whether he is seen by the liberation theologians as a friend of the oppressed, or by some feminist theologians as a gender- specific symbol that encourages attitudes of male dominance, he remains a point of reference for the ethical program of contemporary Christianity.

It is perhaps unnecessary to point out that the social agenda squeezed from the gospels by liberal Protestant, and even more recently Roman Catholic, theologians has no place in the ethical teaching ascribed to Jesus of Nazareth nor in the general biblical understanding of morality. In fact, Jesus of Nazareth lived in a world in which apartheid served as a religious principle and—though the gospels can be cagey on the matter—is not known to have spoken out against the strict laws for- bidding association of Jews with Gentiles. Jesus of Nazareth, however he may be depicted in Hollywood epics grandly conceived by Italian directors, is reckoned to have distanced himself from the major liberation struggle of his day: that of the Jews against their pagan oppressors ("My kingship is not of this world"); the principles of self-determination and democracy were unknown in the stratified Judaism of first-century Palestine, and there is nothing in what Jesus is assumed to have said by the gospel writers that would in the least imply he might have compre- hended such notions if he had come across them. Far from advocating distribution of wealth as a solution to the plight of the poor, Jesus commended poverty as the appropriate preparation for the impending judgment (Luke 6:21; Matt. 26:11), when the enemies of the God would be put on trial and the poor (the "least") would join him in a heavenly banquet (Mark 10:31). Likewise, the Jesus of the gospels is not known to have endorsed the traditional Jewish eudemonia that contemporary readers of the gospel seem to think exists in his teaching. For him, the world is not a source of happiness but of corruption; the present age is the age of Satan and stands already condemned for its inherited wickedness (Mark 18:11f.). The Jesus of the first three gospels does not preach ways around this doom but rather that God's justice will be swift and sure: The heavens and earth are passing away and those within earshot will live to see the final conflagration. Nor is there any stress on prosperity as a sign of divine favor—the other part of the

Judaic eudemonia. Instead, the family is treated as a threat to one's obedience to God (Mark 10:29): one has to be ready to drop one's obligations to it. Rewards for doing so, however, are not to be expected in this world, and hence the truly obedient must expect suffering, persecution, and loss. It is facile to suppose that Jesus' words concerning divisions in families—"I come not to bring peace but a sword"—can be invoked to support defensive wars and revolutions (Matt. 10:34–36); the sword is that of God's judgment, the "divisions" a gratuitous reference to a historical situation that existed only after the death of Jesus and the spread of the missionary movement. It is equally implausible that his words on the occasion of an internal row among his followers, "Be at peace with one another" (Mark 9:49), were meant as a prescription for world peace.

Taken as a whole, the gospel writers are not concerned with Jesus' moral teaching (which, in view of their belief that the world was coming to an end, they would have considered of mere temporary and immediate importance). They are concerned with the supernatural effects of his death. In context, moreover, the teaching assigned to him, when it does not conspicuously serve the purpose of interpreting his death, is of a pedestrian and self-referring sort. It represents the voice of the community grappling with particular issues that have arisen as a result of its changed social and religious situation: whether to pay taxes; whether the leadership of the community is hereditary or elective; whether divorce should and can be procured for reasons other than adultery; whether the laws pertaining to fasting, murder, alms-giving, retaliation, diet, prayer, and marriage are still in effect for people of the new messianic persuasion. The ethics of the New Testament, which we need not generally identify as the ethics of Jesus, are, to borrow a phrase, "situational" if we understand the term to mean a praxis that emerges out of the community's awareness that its original religious homogeneity had been lost, and with it the ability to settle practical and moral difficulties by appeal to the Jewish law and its orthodox interpetations. Paul means nothing other than this when he describes the new pluralism as "a new creation" (2 Cor. 5:17) in which distinctions between Jews and Gentiles are of no importance. That verdict was not easily achieved, however, and neither Paul nor any Synoptic writer can bring himself to endorse what a second-century Christian teacher like Marcion of Sinope finds possible to advocate: the elimination of the Law in its entirety.

The synoptic gospels and the letters of Paul reflect an earlier phase in the crisis of understanding that erupted with the expulsion of the

Christian cults from the synagogues. The ethics of Jesus, as they are portrayed in the gospels, might be expected to reflect a certain cultic bitterness toward this event—which was, after all, the failure of some Jews to persuade other Jews that their beliefs were correct. This accounts for a vituperative tendency in the synoptics to equate goodness with agreement: a good man is one who hears the word, the gospel, or sees the light once hidden, and recognizes it as the truth:

> The good man out of his good treasure brings forth good, and the evil man out of his evil treasure brings forth evil (Matt. 12:35f.).

> You will know them by their fruits; Are grapes gathered from thorns, or figs from thistles? Every sound tree bears good fruit, but the bad tree bears evil fruit. . . . Every tree that does not bear good fruit is cut down and thrown into the fire" (Matt. 7:16ff.).

This is not, as the preachers often frame it, a simplistic comment on "Good is as good does"; it is rather an assertion that those who have not accepted the newfangled messianic preaching belong to a class of people who are—like the bad tree—naturally corrupt. It is not an injunction to moral behavior, therefore, but a bit of polemic against certain kinds of people—imaged elsewhere as barren fig trees, rocky soil, whitewashed tombs, a brood of vipers. The crisis of self-understanding is perhaps even more prominent in Paul's attempts to live without the Law: On the one hand (Rom. 7:6), he can argue that "we are discharged from the law, dead to that which held us captive, so that we serve not under the old written code but in the new life of the spirit." On the other, Paul is consumed with worry over what, on a practical level, life will be like without the code: "Do not use your freedom as an opportunity for sexual pleasure, . . . for the whole law is fulfilled in one phrase: 'Love your neighbor as yourself'" (Gal. 5:13f.). In general, Christian ethics, as we find them especially incorporated into the closing sections of Romans, 1 and 2 Corinthians, and Galatians, are situational in the added sense that they address the needs not of an imperial Christianity nor of a world church, but of relatively isolated pockets of belief scattered throughout Asia Minor, each church (as we may assume from the case of the enthusiasts at Corinth) having a rather different range of moral and practical problems that want solving.

THE IMPORTANCE OF IDENTIFYING CONTEXT

Recognition of the importance of describing the context of any bit of ethical or putatively ethical teaching—the beatitudes, the wisdom-sayings and proverbs assigned to Jesus, the house-rules of the epistles, and the cult rules of the gospels—is widely assumed by biblical scholars. The consequences of failing to do so are just as widely ignored at the pulpit, in seminaries, and by professional theologians, largely, one suspects, because recontextualizing the isolated aphorisms of Jesus and Paul has the undesired effect of marking out the distance between what contemporary believers think Jesus said—as interpreted by the medium of church and Sunday School—and how his sayings were understood by people of his own time. I am aware of a school of literary criticism that regards the distinction between what a text meant in its own time and what it means to a reader in his time as unwholesome, a trait it shares, ironically, with fundamentalist biblical interpretation. But in the case of the gospels, where so much is made to hang on the authority of Jesus' pronouncements, attention must obviously be paid not only to the contemporary appreciation of the sayings assigned to him—whether that appreciation is going to be defined prescriptively, as by the fundamentalists, or existentially, as by the literary scholars—but to the communities and circumstances that produced them. Two examples may suffice to illustrate the importance of describing the original context of an ethical saying:

(a) We are all aware that Jesus is reckoned to have spoken out against wealth. In Luke 12:15 he responds to a question about inheritance by saying "A man's life does not consist in what he owns," and proceeds to tell the story of a man who is slain by God for the rather innocent desire to build bigger barns to store his crops: "He who lays up treasure for himself is not rich toward God." We cannot imagine such a story emerging in Jewish circles, for the simple reason that a man's abundance would not there have been taken as a sign of God's disfavor. At the very least, therefore, the story raises a question about its provenance. What prompted the community responsible for this story so to invert the Jewish eudemonia; what provoked their contempt for the wealthy? A plausible answer is that their insistence on the blessedness of poverty is a reflexive way of making a virtue of social necessity. By and large, the earliest Christians were poor and illiterate; by and large they were rejected by wealthier and better educated Jews. The equation of being poor and being right or moral is the logical consequence of their predicament. A similar story underscores the point:

In Luke 16:19 we find the parable of the rich man who dies and
goes to that very Greek place called Hades. Calling upon Abraham
for mercy, the rich man is reminded, "Son, in your lifetime you received
good things and Lazarus in like manner evil things; but now he is
comforted here and you are in anguish." As if this isn't bad enough,
the rich man is told that he is stuck where he is forever, and that
his rich brothers will in due course join him, despite the rich man's
plea that they would repent of their sins if they knew their fate. The
story ends with Abraham saying, "If they do not hear Moses and the
prophets, neither will they be convinced if someone should rise from
the dead." The target of the tale are the well-to-do who have rejected
the Christian teaching about the resurrection—specifically, those who
have rejected Christian interpretations of the Hebrew Bible in the form
scholars call *testimonia*. It is not a tale about the value of charity,
but about the fate of those who refuse Christian teaching. The list can
be continued: Do not lay up treasures for yourselves on earth; do not
be anxious about what to wear; it is easier for a camel to pass through
the eye of a needle than for a rich man to enter the Kingdom; blessed
are the poor; if you want to be perfect, sell what you have. It would
be very hard indeed to find a single piece of moral teaching so uniformly
attested as Jesus' reputed contempt for wealth and his praise of poverty,
but even harder to imagine a church that would have made a policy
of such contempt. It need hardly be pointed out that neither the Vatican
nor the PTL Club's fun park, Heritage USA, can operate under such
restrictions. In context, this pro-poverty ethic makes sense; it is deeply
rooted in the values of the early community and reflects their particular
sense of what and who is moral: As they are poor and homeless, it
must be the Lord's desire and hence virtuous to be so; the value of
poverty reflects the way in which the community is valued by others.
So seen, there is no practical difficulty in seeing the teaching as being
limited to the circumstances that called it into being. Out of context,
the story of the rich man makes only grim sense. Indeed it is precisely
the distance between a Jesus, who cannot have imagined a time when
his followers would not have been poor and homeless, and the church
of Luke's day, which already showed signs of forgetting its meager origins,
that turned such stories into moral fabliaux. Their later use, except
among the monastics and similar reformist movements, was not considerable. In the imperial church after the fourth century, Jesus' words
about selling one's goods were taken to be a "counsel of perfection,"
an ideal not to be achieved but desired; in short the pro-poverty ethic

was taken to be a matter for allegory and interpretation and not a rule to be obeyed.

(b) The second example of ethical evidence concerns Jesus' supposed attitude toward family obligations. As in the previous case, the sentiment attributed to him would amount to an overturning of the traditionally high value placed on the family in the orthodox Jewish theology of the time. Our source once again is Luke, who in turn is borrowing a saying from a source he evidently shared with the author of Matthew's gospel: "If anyone comes to me and does not hate his own father and mother, wife and children, brothers and sisters, yes—even his own life, he cannot be my disciple" (Luke 14:26f.). Taken at its face value, it is a saying at which almost all reasonable people cringe and one that the church has customarily interpreted as a case of Jesuine hyperbole. Matthew seems to have cringed as well, and so he has rewritten his source as follows: "He who loves his father or mother more than me is not worthy of me and he who loves son and daughter more than me is not worthy of me" (Matt. 10:37). Hating one's family as a precondition of discipleship has been exchanged for the more positive idea of degrees of loving. Given the fact that Matthew's theology is rooted in the Jewish ideal of the family as a religious unit, it is not at all surprising that he was unable to resist altering his source. He was no fundamentalist. But here again, the decision to accept the teaching at face value (and here there are two face values) must depend on our awareness of historical context and an appreciation of why the early Christians assigned such sayings to Jesus. Those reasons are not beyond historical discovery, but they are tied to the special interests of the earliest church. In this instance, the counsel of Jesus is best understood if we see in his utterance the alienation that followed when families and synagogues divided over whether to embrace the messianic preaching of wandering missionaries. It will have been a predictable part of missionary preaching to supply a meaning for those divisions, and nothing provides meaning in meaningless or ambiguous situations like the notion that an unforeseen consequence was in fact foreseen. In this case, Jesus is credited with endorsing such conflict not as a simple result of family quarrelling, but as the mark of true discipleship. Yet here, as in the case of the pro-poverty ethic, the teaching is construed after the fact as a way of explaining an existing and potentially hurtful situation to new believers, believers newly cut asunder from their religious past and practice.

An awareness of historical context may help us, in the long run, to avoid the twin dangers of oversimplification, and allegorization.

Oversimplification leads to something like this: If Jesus said hate your family and love your enemies, then his ethics are beastly and we can well do without them. Allegorization of the ethic is equally amiss, though it has kept Christian theology in business for a very long time: Jesus can not have meant what it seems he meant; he did not mean by "hate" what we mean, since he spoke with the mind of God and was drawing the minds of his disciples to the sublime promise of God. What he said was a divine mystery. Context will not make an ethic palatable, but it will save one from naive assumptions about what is often perceived as the difficulty and severity of Jesus' moral demands.

CHRISTIANITY AND MOSES

Before their expulsion from the synagogue, the earliest Christians would have had no call to question the relevance of the Mosaic Code; after that separation there is virtually no part of Christian ethical teaching that does not in some way reflect their sense of religious alienation and ambiguity.

In an overstressed portion of Matthew's gospel (5:17) Jesus is actually represented as prescribing that code for the church. Tradition is fluid, however, and the ethnocentrism of Matthew is both internally (that is, editorially, cf. 10:5 and 10:18) and externally weakened by stories about how Jesus and later his followers challenged and were freed from the requirements of the Law. Having successfully—by which I mean strategically—satisfied themselves that the Law was a dead letter—that which, as Paul puts it, brings about knowledge of sin—it was a small matter to construct the interim ethic that we find given to Jesus in chiefly the first three gospels. The term *interim ethic* is a typical bit of theological jargon, used by biblical scholars to suggest that the early church did not manage or desire to create an ethic for the future. Their apocalyptic hopes would have prevented it. A world under judgment, like the world of the gospels, is in need of salvation, not a new moral order. Hence, the ethics of Paul and Jesus must be viewed against the background of the apocalyptic vision that they shared with their converts.

That vision—the judgment of the world and the salvation of a few—was not a perspective that lent itself easily to ethical construction. It follows that whatever ethical code Christian interpreters later extracted and pieced together from the discrete books of the New Testament needed the coherence of the ethical code of the Christian Old Testament.

There it was a covenant with specific geopolitical terms and consequences. In the Old Testament we have not merely ethics but Law, both of a casuistic and apodictic variety: Do not do this; do this and that must happen; do evil and harm will come to the whole nation. The sense that sin and guilt can be imputed to a whole people (as in the New Testament idea that the sins of the people can be imputed to a perfectly righteous man and atoned for in his death) are part and parcel of the covenantal theology. In the Jewish view of Jesus' day the world is a bad place not *because* Satan makes it so but because people cannot keep God's commands. Paul, drawing on a minor theme in rabbincal interpretation, makes certain guesses about *why* people cannot keep the law, and concludes that Satan's proprietorship of the world is to blame: it has created a general state of moral evil from which no one—neither Jew nor Gentile—is free. In the Jewish view, we have what is essentially a civil code with divine authorization, as well as a way of accounting for the sorry state of the nation, the existence of poverty, the prevalence of disease and early death, even of the wickedness of the powerful: People do wrong things and cause other people pain. The primary focus for Jews—unlike the Pauline Christians—was not on the God of Genesis and his quarrel with the powers of darkness, but on the God of Abraham and Moses—God the code-giver, and in the correctness of one's life (righteousness is the preferred term) as measured against that code. It is necessary to stress that this emphasis on correctness is not convertible with morality; adhering to the law, then as now, keeps one out of trouble, but adherence to (for example) the marriage laws or the dietary laws, on a practical level, differed from modern income tax law only in terms of the presumed source of the code.

As is well known, there is considerable ranting against the concept of technical righteousness in the prophetic literature (e.g., Jer. 31:33; Hos. 10:4) and it is an arguably reliable tradition that the followers of Jesus, if not Jesus himself, were impugned for failing *inter alia* to fast, wash, choose their table companions carefully, and for healing and gathering provisions on the Sabbath. The clincher in Mark's gospel is the suggestion that Jesus came to call not the righteous but the sinner (Mark 2:17). The import of such a suggestion is enormously difficult to grasp as an indictment of the Jewish understanding of technical righteousness when we consider that Jesus speaks in the same passage of the righteous as being "healthy" and the sinner as "sick," which is to say those who stand in a correct relationship with the Law have no need of him. Paul can only have shuddered at such a distinction. In short, the New Testament writers point behind them to a time when there was considerable uncertainty about how one could be moral if one were not also "correct" *vis-à-vis* the law. Despairing of teaching the finer points of the Law to those he calls the uncircumcized, and pressed by the desire to outdo the other apostles in the race for converts, Paul is eventually persuaded to reject the demand (still then in use among Jewish Christians) for adherence to the Law and to emphasize instead the simplicity of faith, which he combines with the quasi-ethical construct of "Love of neighbor" as an epitome of the whole Mosaic Code. Christians have always seen Paul's accommodation to the Gentiles as the very essence of Christian ethical teaching, though there is nothing originally Christian about it, and it flies in the face of Jesus' attributively more kosher attitude: "Let your righteousness exceed that of the Pharisees. Whoever teaches men to wipe away even the least of the commandments shall be called least in the Kingdom of God." Alas for Paul, judged by those standards.

As a cumulative matter, the idea of technical righteousness according to a legal code, is set aside in the New Testament on the reckoning that God is working in new ways, not to procure right conduct of a disobedient people, but to save people from the metaphysical condition—Paul calls it the "old man"—which makes disobedience prevalent. It was the profound insight of Augustine and later Luther that taught us what Paul meant: He meant, said Augustine, that not being able not to sin was the natural condition of humanity, a condition from which we cannot save ourselves. The Jewish idea of objective guilt for objective wrongdoing and conspicuous reward for conspicuous rightdoing were transformed by Paul (to a lesser extent by the gospel writers) into the pessimistic doctrine that later generations would know by the name Original Sin—an inherent disposition always to do what is wrong: "I am carnal. Sold under sin I do not understand my own actions. I do not do what I want but the very thing I hate . . . and doing what I do not want to do, it is not I that do it but sin which dwells in me. For I know that nothing good dwells within me—that is in my own flesh. I can will what is right, but I cannot do it. For I do not do the good I want, but the evil I do not want is what I do. Now, if I do what I do not want, it is no longer I that do it, but sin which dwells in me" (Rom. 7:14–20). Before moving away from this passage, we should be clear that Paul is not the whole of the New Testament and there is only an inkling of this abdication of moral responsibility in the synoptic gospels. G. B. Shaw, in commenting on the difference between the teaching of Paul and Jesus in his preface to *Androcles and the Lion,* emphasized that we cannot imagine the Jesus who instructs the woman taken in adultery to "sin no more" saying instead, "Go ahead and sin all you like; I'm gonig to take care of it anyway." And while this may be a mere literary man's appraisal of a thorny theological problem, it is considerably closer to the distinction between what German scholars used to call Petrine and Pauline Christianity that many theologians have appreciated.

What is ever-present in the Old Testament is the perception of God's ongoing relationship with a people. The system of rewards and punishments is this-worldly; blessing—as in the case of Abraham and Job—is not a metaphysical condition of the soul but a return on one's investment in the Law. This covenantal relationship is missing in the interim ethics of the New Testament or, more exactly, it is exchanged for a relationship that no longer recognizes the objective value of keeping the Law. This is even the case in the much-touted passage already quoted from Matthew 5:17f., where, in any event, keeping the law is not seen as a way to this-worldly prosperity but as a means by which to gain rank in the world to come. Israel, like the fig tree that Jesus curses, the Temple that he "cleanses," the twelve tribes to be judged by his twelve apostles, or the elder brother of the prodigal son, is no longer an object of his care or concern. This might suggest to us that the chauvinism of the Christians in expounding their vision of the new age and of themselves as God's elect will have had a direct bearing on the sorts of ethical teaching their writings include.

As the ethics of the Old Testament are centered on the idea of covenant, the ethics of the New Testament are centered on the plight of people who reject it. Psychologically and historically, it is really the rejection of their salvationist doctrine by the Jews that finally shapes the terms of Christian repudiation of the Law, a fact nowhere more eloquently witnessed than in Paul's Letter to the Romans where he struggles with his fellow Jews and his own instincts to suggest finally the distinction between doing right and being saved. Being saved is cosmological necessity since the world is being closed down; Satan is losing strength and salvation is at hand. In the time before the end there are things that the people of God might do as a reflection of having received God's grace: Hate what is evil, hold to what is good, love one another, outdo one another in showing courtesy, contribute to each others' needs, bless those who persecute you, repay no one evil for evil, do not be conceited, never avenge yourselves, weep with those who weep, be subject to the governing authorities since they have their power from God, pay taxes, owe no one anything, and so on. As for the Law: "The commandments you shall not kill, steal, or covet are summed up in this sentence: 'You shall love your neighbor as yourself.' Love is thus the fulfilling of the whole Law" (Rom. 13, epitomized). Much of what is unarguably noble and wise comes in these incidental passages in Paul's letters. Yet it is precisely these passages, including the love-ethic itself, which have the least claim to being distinctively Christian. They are the garden-variety platitudes of the late Hellenistic world, and one can find them scattered throughout the work of ancient historians, playwrights, and orators, and in the Jewish proverbial and wisdom literature.

To summarize what is now at the point of becoming obvious from these reflections on the gospels and letters of the New Testament, the sacred book of Christianity is not chiefly about ethics. Such ethical teaching as the New Testament contains is of an occasional variety and reflects situations within the embryonic church of the first and early second centuries of the common era. Those situations, we need to remind ourselves, are largely unfamiliar to modern readers and the solutions proposed by the gospel writers for dealing with them are as distant from us—and hence potentially as irrelevant for us—as the situations which called them into being.

6

On Slavery
Biblical Teaching v. Modern Morality

Morton Smith

I suppose we all agree in finding slavery repulsive. Although we should grant that some people need direction or want strong figures on whom to rely, yet we would reject the notion that one person should actually own another as one owns an animal or a piece of furniture, with freedom to dispose of it at any time. Such a relationship, we should say, denies the essential dignity—the basic humanity—of a human being. It is not only an outrage to the slave, but a disgrace to the owner because it reveals his lack of moral feeling.

This attitude, however, as we all know, is comparatively new. A little over a century ago, this very city was the capital of a great confederacy formed, among other purposes, to defend the ownership of slaves. Our present position is the consequence, not only of the terrible war that broke the power of the confederacy, but also of a century-long campaign of moral education and social and political organization that culminated in that war and by means of it succeeded in changing both the laws and the public opinion that permitted slavery.

Among the reasons that made the campaign so long and so difficult was the fact that slavery is not only permitted, but actually ordained by the Bible. The first biblical mention of it, in fact, prescribes it for a whole third of mankind—the descendants of Ham, the son of Noah.

You may remember the story told in Genesis 6-9. Noah was the only man God liked well enough to save from the flood (Gen. 6:8,13f.).

Morton Smith is professor emeritus of ancient history at Columbia University.

After the flood, however, he took to drink and lay drunk and naked in his tent. His son Ham saw him in this condition and told his two brothers, Shem and Japeth. They took a cloak between them, went into the tent backwards, and covered Noah without seeing him. When Noah woke up he learned that Ham had told on him and consequently cursed Ham's descendants in the person of his son, Canaan, saying, "Let him be a slave of slaves" (Gen. 9:18-27). Since, according to biblical legend, all mankind was descended from these three boys, Noah's course destined a third of mankind to be enslaved to the others. This is the interpretation of the story indicated by its context (Gen. 1–11), which is full of such legends of events that led somebody to say something that became a rule for all time thereafter; thus, for instance, God reportedly told the snake that it would go about on its belly, and the woman that she would have pain in childbirth, and Adam that he would live by labor, and these all became permanent rules (Gen. 3:14, 16, 19), and so on.

The translators of the Authorized Version were a bit embarrassed by Noah's curse. Jerome, who knew Hebrew, had translated it accurately, *servus servorum,* but the Greek translation, though it also meant "slave" (*pais oiketēs*), was in less familiar words and did not follow the Hebrew exactly, so the Englishmen compromised and made it "servant of servants." Consequently I have to comment on the sense of the Hebrew text.

Biblical Hebrew is poor in words that express social relationships. It uses one term, *'eved,* for any kind of servant, from a king's minister (2 Kings 25:8; etc.) to a nomad's slave (Gen. 12:16). The primary sense, however, is "slave"; the other senses are metaphorical. So, for example, is the use in polite address when the speaker refers to himself as "your slave." (Here, as above, English usage replaced "slave" with "servant," so until World War II old fashioned Englishmen went on signing themselves, "Your humble and obedient servant."[1]) The words for "female slave" were similarly ambiguous.[2] Therefore to determine the sense of one of these words in a particular case, one must always consider the context. Likewise, to determine the actual conditions of slaves throughout the centuries in which the Biblical books were written, one must look at the contexts of all those passages in which these words refer to slaves.

These tasks would be much too long for this paper. Let me take only one early and famous example, the story of Abraham, Sarah, and Hagar, which shows how a tenth-or ninth-century B.C. Israelite author thought his pious hero would treat a slave girl (Gen. 16:1–16; 21:8-21). As everybody knows, Abraham and his half-sister Sarah had long lived in—shall we say, "half-incestuous marriage." Sarah, however, was childless. She had some property of her own, among it, some slave girls, and she decided to give one of them to Abraham so that he could have children from her former property. She thought this would, as she put it, "build her up" (16:2). Her choice was an Egyptian girl, Hagar, whom she may have bought while visiting Egypt some ten years before. Abraham was well on in years,[3] but of course no question was asked of how the girl would like it. Sarah simply put the proposition to Abraham; he agreed; she gave him Hagar; Hagar conceived and then became contemptuous of Sarah. Sarah complained to Abraham and he said, in effect, "I give her back to you;[4] do as you like with her." Sarah treated her so badly that she ran away, but when she got out into the desert she saw an angel who advised her to go back, take her medicine and keep her place. After all, she had Abraham's child in her, so she could not be treated too badly, and the child might grow up to avenge her. (It is remarkable how often visions give basically sensible advice.) She obeyed and had the child—a boy who was called Ishmael—and then, some thirteen years later, Sarah had a son. No sooner was Sarah's son weaned than she saw Ishmael as a possible competitor for a share in Abraham's property. Sarah then demanded that Abraham drive Hagar and Ishmael out of the camp. Abraham did not want to "because of his son" (nothing is said of any concern about Hagar, [21:11]), but another prudent angel advised him to do as Sarah demanded, so he did. Hagar had probably been a slave in the family for more than twenty years. When big-hearted Abraham sent her away he gave her some bread and a jug of water so large that she had to carry it on her shoulder (21:14). With this parting gift she and her son were sent off on foot into the desert.

This story indicates clearly the social status of what the Authorized Version politely called Sarah's "handmaid." The proper term is "slave," and the social practices that the Bible takes for granted, without any criticism, are those of chattel slavery. Hagar was simply a piece of property, to be used as needed and thrown out when needed no longer.

Strong's *Exhaustive Concordance*[5] indicates that, in the whole Bible, the Authorized Version uses "slave" only twice, and the Revised Version only twice more, though there are hundreds of uses of Greek and Hebrew words with the meaning "slave." Stories like the preceding, that would illustrate the meaning, are vivid, but necessarily deal with particular cases. Let us therefore turn to laws, which give a better picture of general practices.

According to the Bible, slaves might be acquired by capture in war (e.g., Deut. 20:10ff.), or they might be purchased from slave dealers or resident aliens. The author of Leviticus so much preferred these latter methods of acquisition that he made the use of them a positive commandment (25:44ff.): "From the gentiles who are round about you, from them *you shall buy* male and female slaves, and also from the descendants of the natives who are living with you, from them *you shall buy,* and from their descendants . . . and (the slaves purchased) shall be your (permanent) possessions; you shall bequeath them to your children after you as a permanent possession forever; you shall use them as slaves."

While prescribing this treatment for gentiles, Leviticus discouraged the purchase of Israelite slaves, but did not prohibit it. The context of the passage just cited, and many other texts, make it clear that there were poor men willing to sell off their children, or even to sell themselves, for slaves, and even Israelites and their children might be purchased, though their condition after purchase was mitigated by some special laws (Exod. 21; Deut. 15; Num. 25). Defaulting debtors, also, could be seized by creditors and sold into slavery (2 Kings 4:1; Neh. 5:1-5), sometimes, reportedly, for as little as the price of a pair of shoes (Amos 2:6—though prophetic rhetoric, then as now, is not wholly trustworthy). Similarly, thieves who could not pay for what they had stolen were enslaved (Exod. 22:2). Finally, an owner could breed slaves from his own stock. The Bible says, "If (an Israelite slave's) master gives him (a slave woman as) a wife and she bears him sons or daughters, the wife and her children shall belong to the master." If the Israelite slave is set free, "he shall go out by himself" (Exod. 21:4). In the same way, any other property a slave might acquire belonged to his master. For instance, after David became king he gave the son of Jonathan, his former lover, all that remained of Saul's property, including one of Saul's slaves named Ziba. Ziba had fifteen sons and twenty slaves of his own, so all these, along with him, became slaves of Jonathan's son (2 Sam. 9:1-10).

The extent of the master's property rights is perhaps best shown by the law on manslaughter. If two free men fight and, during the fight, one kills the other, the winner is also to be killed, but if the loser survives for a day or two and gets up and walks about, the winner need pay him only for his loss of time. On the other hand, if a man beats his slave so that the slave dies during the beating, the law is only that the slave "shall be avenged" (Exod. 21:20)—the vengeance is not specified—and (the text goes on) "if (the slave) survives for a day or two he shall not be avenged, for he is his (master's) property," literally "his money" (Exod. 21:21).

On all these matters the texts are reasonably clear. Consequently, if we take the Old Testament literally, we must admit that, as one American preacher put it in 1857, "slavery is of God."[6]

I suppose a number of Christians will have gone along with all of this complacently, in the expectation of pointing out that the Mosaic law was somehow or other "fulfilled" by Jesus and this "fulfilment" somehow or other invalidated it, so that, from then on, it was to be read with profound respect and regarded with profound indifference. Something like this may have been the position of Paul. Luckily, however, we need not discuss that question. Let us, for the sake of the argument, concede the claim, throw out the Old Testament and its embarrassing laws, and consider only what the New Testament has to say about slavery.

It has to say it in Greek, therefore what it says is fairly clear, because the Greek word *doulos,* meaning "slave," has little of the ambiguity of the Hebrew *'eved.* So far as I know, until Christians got control of the Roman Empire, *doulos* was never used of a king's minister, nor by a free man in self depreciation, except in translations of Near Eastern texts (among them, the Old Testament)[7] or in speaking of enslavement to the gods.[8] When otherwise used of free men it is pejorative—indicating subjugation, usually moral or political—a "slave" of the passions, a "subject" of the Persian King, and the like. While slaves and free men may be referred to alike as "servants," "helpers," and so on, the difference of legal status remains sharp. When a free servant is called a *doulos* the speaker is either abusing him or mistaken.[9] This clarity has been completely obscured in the Authorized and Revised Versions of the New Testament, which commonly translate *doulos* as "servant" or the like, as part of their practice of whitewashing the Word of God.

Once these facts are clear, we can see that Jesus lived in a world where slavery was common. There were innumerable slaves of the emperor and of the Roman state; the Jerusalem temple owned slaves; the High Priests owned slaves (one of them lost an ear in Jesus' arrest), all of the rich and almost all of the middle class owned slaves. So far as we are told, Jesus said nothing against this. He took the state of affairs for granted and shaped his parables accordingly. In those, as in real life, the great men, whether they represent God or the devil, are usually slave owners and the main problem for their slaves, as Jesus presents things, is not to get free, but to win their master's praise.[10] There seem to have been slave revolts in Palestine and Jordan in Jesus' youth

(Josephus, *Bellum* 2:55–65); a miracle-working leader of such a revolt would have attracted a large following; if Jesus had denounced slavery or promised liberation we should almost certainly have heard of his doing so. We hear nothing, so the most likely supposition is that he said nothing. (The silence cannot plausibly be explained by supposing that he kept the teaching secret, or that his followers suppressed it. We know that both he and they employed not only secrecy but suppression regarding his claim to be King of the Jews and with respect to his magical practices. Nevertheless, reports of both Messianic claims and magical rites have come down to us.[11]) Had there been any considerable teaching or significant action about liberation of slaves, reports of that would have reached us, too. The issue was a hot one.

Also, if he had advocated liberation his adherents would probably have followed his teaching. But the gospels and Acts say nothing of it, and Paul, our earliest Christian writer (a whole generation before the gospels) not merely tolerates slavery, but orders Christians to continue it. He has the notion, perhaps from Jesus' magical practice, that all those baptized "into Jesus" are united with their Savior, so that "in" Him "there is neither slave nor free, there is neither male nor female, but all . . . are one in Messiah Jesus" (Gal. 3:28; cf. Rom. 10:12; 1 Cor. 7:22; 12:13; Col. 3:11). However, Paul recognizes that this internal union does not obliterate differences of social position in the outside world. Though he thinks these differences relatively unimportant, he insists that they continue. Of slavery in particular he says, "If you, as a slave, were called (by God, to become a Christian), don't worry (about your slavery), but if you can also become a free man, you had better. . . . (As a general rule, however,) let each man remain in that (social position) in which he was called" (1 Cor. 7:21, 24).

What this meant in practice was shown when one of the slaves of Philemon (a convert) ran away, came to Paul, and was converted by him. This conversion put Paul in a tight spot. To conceal a runaway slave was legally a theft,[12] and the penalties were severe. So he sent the slave back to Philemon, with a letter to him, asking him as a favor to keep the slave "forever, no longer (as) a slave, but. . . (as) a beloved brother." The letter concludes, "Confident of your obedience, I have written you, knowing that you will do even more than I say. And at the same time prepare accommodations for me, for I hope to visit you soon." This was a gentle way of telling Philemon that Paul intended to check up on what would be done to the slave. The whole letter, in fact, is wonderfully kind and careful, and this increases the significance of what it carefully does *not* say. It does *not* say, "Christians are not allowed to own each other as slaves; therefore, by conversion, your slave has become free of you." On the contrary, it recognizes the validity of Philemon's ownership of the slave and hopes that he will continue to *own* (Greek, *apechein*) him forever. But it asks him, please, as a special favor, to treat *this* slave as a brother.[13] Of course Philemon's ownership and treatment of his other slaves, particularly those who are pagans, is not questioned. Neither is slavery as an institution; its validity is implicitly recognized.

If there were any doubt about the meaning of the letter to Philemon, it would be settled by the letter to the Colossians, if only we were sure that Colossians were genuine. But even if it were not, it would certainly be the earliest, closest, and most perceptive imitation and interpretation of Paul. After laying down the Pauline rule that "in Christ" "there is neither Greek nor Jew . . . barbarian, Scythian, slave (or) free man" (3:11), Colossians goes on to give rules of behavior for persons in different social positions: wives, husbands, children, parents, then, "Slaves, be obedient in all things to your civil (Greek, *kata sarka*) masters, not with pretended obedience like those trying to please men, but sincerely, fearing the Lord. . . . You serve the Lord Messiah and any cheater will get what (he deserves)" (3:22-25). Whether or not the master is Christian is not asked. Simply as owner he is, by civil law, in the place of God—though the text goes on to warn owners that they must be just and evenhanded in dealing with their slaves, knowing that they themselves have a master in heaven (4:1). This picture of the entire world as a great Roman estate of which all the inhabitants are the slaves of God, the owner, was not peculiarly Christian. Even before the church won legal acceptance the emperors were beginning to take the title "master" (*dominus*) proper to the head of the household and owner of the slaves. However, the triumph of Christianity did much to strengthen the trend and, among the elements of Christianity, Paul's habitual designation of himself as "Paul, the slave of Christ" (Rom. 1:1; Gal. 1:10; Phil. 1:1; imitated in Titus 1:1; etc.) was particularly influential. This loathsome belief, that man is properly a slave, obviously invites rhetorical development, so we go back at once to the simpler question, What does the New Testament say about actual slavery?

Colossians was often imitated, so the New Testament contains a number of generally recognized, pseudo-Pauline forgeries, and three of these, Ephesians, 1 Timothy, and Titus, contain passages on slavery,[14] to the same effect as the one we have just seen. Of these, 1 Timothy is most interesting because it particularly enjoins Christian slaves to obey Christian masters, who are "not to treat them contemptuously just because they are brothers" (in Christ).

With all these clear passages, there is no reasonable doubt that the New Testament, like the Old, not only tolerated chattel slavery (the form prevalent in the Greco-Roman world of Paul's time), but perpetuated it by making the slaves' obedience to their masters a religious duty. This biblical morality was one of the great handicaps that the emancipation movement in this country had to overcome.[15] That it was overcome, and that revulsion to slavery is now, in this country, almost universal, is one of our great national accomplishments, one for which we have to thank not only common decency and common sense, but also the pagan, classical tradition in our higher education that perpetuated the Greek and Roman eulogies of liberty, and also the wide-spread and healthy indifference of our rationalistic ancestors to the teachings of the Bible. Benjamin Franklin and Thomas Paine are justly remembered among our great national educators.

NOTES

1. Compare with the papal *servus servorum dei*.

2. *Shiphah* and *'amah*. For the use of the former in polite self-deprecation see 2 Sam. 14:7-19.

3. The Bible makes him eight-five (Gen. 16:16), an unusually gifted man.

4. This is the legal significance of the Hebrew, "Behold, your slave girl is in your hand" (Gen. 16:6).

5. J. Strong, *The Exhaustive Concordance of the Bible*, Madison, N. J., 1894.

6. F. Ross, *Slavery Ordained of God*, Philadelphia, 1857, p. 5.

7. This includes texts that are virtually translations, e.g., Josephus, *Antiquities* 2:70.

8. E.g. Luke. 1:38, and numerous pagan uses. When Paul describes himself as a slave of the Corinthians "for Jesus' sake" (2 Cor. 4:5) the enslavement is clearly to Jesus. So, too, Matt. 20:27, etc. Notice that the free, hired laborers who receive pay are not "slaves" but "workers," Matt. 10:10; 20:1-8; James 5:4; etc.

9. Similarly Paul's description of a child as "no different from a slave" is deliberately contemptuous (of pre-Christian Judaism)—Gal. 4:1.

10. Matt. 10:25, a good slave should do as his master; 18:23-35; 24:45-50; 25:14-30; Mark 13:34-36; Luke 7:2-10; 12:42-47; 17:7-10; 19:12-26; John 13:1f.; 15:14-17.

11. See M. Smith, *Jesus the Magician*, Harper and Row, San Francisco, 1981.

12. A. Berger, *Encyclopedic Dictionary of Roman Law*, Philadelphia, 1953 (Am. Philos. Soc. *Transactions* NS 43.2), p. 705.

13. Paul probably had in mind, but significantly did not cite, the passage of

Leviticus from which 25:44ff. was cited above. That passage distinguishes sharply between Gentiles, who are to be enslaved, and "your brother" the Israelite, who, even if enslaved, is to be treated kindly.

14. 1 Tim. 6:1–2; Eph. 6:5–8; Titus 2:9–10.

15. Amusing examples of attempts to explain away the biblical facts will be found in, e.g., A. Barnes, *An Inquiry into the Scriptural Views of Slavery,* N.Y., 1857, *passim;* J. Blanchard and N. Rice, *A Debate on Slavery,* Cincinnati and New York, 1846, 248-419; R. Sunderland, *Anti-Slavery Manual,* N.Y., 1837, chs. 7-9.

7

The Book of Job
The Wisdom of Hebraic Stoicism

Lewis S. Feuer

The great contribution of the Book of Job to wisdom is that it refuted utterly the theology of guilt that the prophets advocated. Proverbs had been concerned with the homely prudence of everyday life, and left aside questions of politics; Ecclesiastes, emphasizing the aspect of the eternal sameness in social existence and the waves of historical movements, placed its veto on all grandiose projects for reconstructing social relations. Such efforts at social revolution only added more pain and turbulence. Job, on the other hand, confuted for all time the claim that the evils men suffer are their just chastisement by God for the sins they have indubitably perpetrated. Though the experience of guilt, let us acknowledge at the outset, is intrinsic to a humane life, it pertains ethically only to those actions for which we are, in some degree, responsible; there can be no moral guilt founded simply on the fact of our human birth. By contrast, theologies of guilt regard it as inherent either in man's biological origin, or the duplicity or stupidity of our putative ancestors. How deep this theology of guilt permeates our attitudes was shown most poignantly during the years 1933–1935 when Hitler's Nazis were entrenching themselves in positions of power; the Jews in Germany, experiencing the Nazi repressions, finding themselves often imprisoned, their children driven from schools, and their goods seized, turned to their philosophers for counsel; then the distinguished Martin Buber told them, as Bildad the Shuhite told Job, to remember

---

Lewis S. Feuer is professor emeritus of sociology at the University of Virginia.

their own guilt, their greed, their cleverness: "No one is free from guilt, no one may exclude himself from it," and rather than justify themselves, they should search within themselves, and engage in confession.[1]

The theology of guilt has indeed tended to disorient the rational understanding and undermine the rational will during times of historical crises. The Hebrew prophets had justified the crushing of the kingdoms of Israel and Judea by the armies of Assyria and Babylonia; the sins of the Hebrew tribes, they claimed, required the retribution of their political and economic destruction, and subsequent exile. There were many, however, who felt that the higher ethic of the Hebrews had not availed against the bigger brigades and catapults of the Babylonians, and challenged the proposition that God is just. The legend of Job, the exemplar of an upright man, therefore posed an ideal crucial experiment for the theory that human misery is inflicted by a just God. Job, having sustained a series of calamities to his family and fortune, reduced to naught, humiliated by boils on his body and a wife who advised him to die, refuses to condemn himself; instead, he indicts God as the Author of Evil. Sustaining all ignominies, Job refuses to allow his integrity to be broken; he will not recede into the masochist pattern of self-reproach for sins unknown. Instead, he curses a human existence that is imbued with injustice and degradation: "Let the day perish wherein I was born, and the night wherein it was said, a man child is brought forth." With those same words, Jude, the obscure Joban hero of Thomas Hardy's agnostic humanist novel, himself finally rejects the terms of personal existence. There is no preachment of man's original sin in Job; the pathetically infantile myth of Adam's sin and its purported consequences does not mar its pages; there is no fantasy that Adam's sin was original, and all subsequent sins unoriginal. Above all, Job never yields to a God-broken frame of mind, and concedes that he has ever engaged in sinful deeds of human exploitation.

The rabbis who edited the scriptures and decided which books were to be included and which excluded were much troubled by the Book of Job. One of them charged that "Job sought to exculpate the whole world," and held God Himself responsible for having created "both evil and righteous men." Another maintained that God always counterposed to every evil He created a corresponding good: "If God created the evil inclination, he also created the Torah as its antidote." Above all, they felt that Job was presumptuous and rebellious in daring to argue with God as an equal: "Dust should be put in the mouth of Job, because he made himself the colleague of heaven. . . ; is there a servant who argues with his master?" Others refused to credit Job's assertion that he was sinless; if with his lips he had not sinned, said one famed authority, "he did sin with his heart."[2] Nonetheless, the Book of Job managed to be included in the last collection, the *Ketuvim* (Writings), that were finally accepted as canonical by the generation before the destruction of the Second Temple.[3]

The Book of Job, remarkable for the fact that its hero is a non-Hebrew, one of the "children of the East," thus stood honorably in the scriptures with its perpetual challenge to the prophetic monotheism, with indeed, its familiar "masochistic" overtones. For the prophets, Amos, Isaiah, Jeremiah, were great scolders, blamers, accusers, like their six-teenth-century spiritual successor, John Calvin, who was aptly called by his fellow-students the "accusative case." Bildad the Shuhite, one of Job's three comforting and arguing friends, similarly sought to rebuke Job for his latent guilt: "How then can man be just with God? or how can he be clean that is born of a woman?. . . ."[4] From what social perspective, however, was the Book of Job with its critique of the theology of guilt then written? Was there any new political conception that the Book of Job subserved? Job indeed goes freely, as a non-Hebrew, beyond the bounds of the covenants with Abraham, Jacob, and Moses. He has ceased to be a tribal ideologist, and become the first universal phi-losopher in the Bible; he proclaims the autonomous conscience; if God is punishing him, He is unjust. He finds no sin in himself, and, unlike Thomas Hobbes, the English philosopher, he refuses to equate God's power with the meaning of justice.[5] And Job, in effect, thus refuses to acknowledge that the supernatural is necessarily divine; only when the supernatural is purged of its impersonal cruelty can it be regarded as divine. He perceives that man's relationship with God, whatever it might be, is not that of a dialogue:

Oh that I had one to hear me!—
Lo, here is my signature, let the Almighty answer me—
And that I had the indictment which mine adversary hath written![6]

Scholars have sought to relate the Book of Job to the social conflicts arising in Judea beginning with the fourth century B.C.E. The distin-guished scholar Louis Finkelstein argued that Job spoke for the plebeians (the lower class), for "a whole philosophic group" among them who would not acknowledge that their misery was the consequence of their own impiety.[7] On the other hand, Job, a prosperous pastoralist but

charitable to the poor and a judge in the town tribunal, is depicted
as having been overthrown from his high position by some social uprising
supported by the youth. A fallen political chieftain, defeated despite
his devotion to the people, he is now disillusioned, as he sees himself
despised and rejected:

> I was a father to the needy, and the cause of him that
> I knew not I searched out.
> And I broke the jaws of the unrighteous, and plucked the
> prey out of his teeth. (29:16, 17)

> When I went forth to the gate unto the city, When I prepared
> my seat in the broad place,
> The young men saw me, and hid themselves: and the aged
> rose up and stood. (29:7, 8)

Possibly a plebeian movement, one of the lowest class, arose and
expropriated or destroyed the possessions of this urban Job, rather than
as the older legend would have it: that he lost his flocks and houses
entirely at the hands of Sabean and Chaldean marauders. Perhaps the
new subversives were led by men of a new generation:

> Upon my right hand rise the brood (Youth); they entangle
> my feet, and they cast up against me their ways of destruction.
> (30:12)

Job's resentment and contempt are kindled not only against these
youthful subversives but also, and perhaps uncharitably, against the
fathers who nurtured them:

> But now they that are younger than I have me in derision,
> whose fathers I disdained to have set with the dogs of my flock.
> (30:1)

Quite obviously, the "brood (Youth)" would have had no cause
for deriding Job if his downfall had simply been the result of foreign
marauding bands, for the latter inflicted misfortune upon all alike as
they chose. Evidently the Youth itself had had a role in overthrowing
Job and, like all revolutionaries, relished their adversary's collapse. The
hypothesis therefore suggests itself, similar to that proposed by Robert

Gordis, that Job reflected an upper-class viewpoint that was common to all the Wisdom writers, the outlook of the wealthy and prudent, suspicious of advocates for social change,[8] and like the later Sadducees, disbelievers in the immortality of the soul: "If a man die, may he live again?" (14:14). On the other hand, in two respects Job clearly ventures far beyond the wisdom of Ecclesiastes and Proverbs. For one, he takes to heart the misery of the poor, and actively intervenes in their behalf. He assails the enclosure movement, the forfeitures of mortgaged land: "There are those that remove the landmarks; they violently take away flocks, and feed them" (24:2). "He lieth down rich . . .; he openeth his eyes, and his wealth is not" (27:19). And Job is moved by the troubled ones: "If I have not wept for him that was in trouble? And, if my soul grieved not for the needy" (30:25); he provides them with clothing, as he provided lodgings for the stranger (31:19, 24, 32). If Job's social outlook seems akin to that of a philanthropic Tory radical, the Youth, who deride him are the indifferent children of the well-to-do, akin to a pleasure-loving "jeunesse dorée."

Secondly, Job, as the first cosmopolitan hero in the Bible, as a non-Hebrew, appeals to a universal God, not the God of some people or tribe, but solely the transtribal, transnational God who is all-powerful, and presumably all-good. As such, the Book of Job may have expressed the cosmopolitan movement that first appeared among Jews in all classes with the advent of Alexander the Great, when Jews responded to the noble aspiration, the promise of a peaceful world, commercial prosperity, the advancement of science and learning, and the equality of all people that the Macedonian imperialist was the first to bring with him. Jews of all classes and all ages welcomed the young Alexander. According to the legend recorded by Flavius Josephus, Alexander was benevolently inclined toward the Jews; when he first beheld their high priest, he exclaimed that he had dreamt of "the very person" when he was still in Macedonia considering how to embark upon his campaign for "the dominion of Asia," and that this person had exhorted him "to make no delay, . . . I believe that I bring this army under the divine conduct, and shall therewith conquer Darius, and destroy the power of the Persian, ..."[9] The new philosophy of mankind that Alexander brought with him, and that had been lacking under the Persian rule, stirred young Jews so much that (according to Josephus) many of them joined the army of Alexander as volunteers, while he, in turn promised that when the Babylonian Jews were liberated, they would "enjoy their own laws." Jews named their sons after Alexander.

The tremendous popular response of the Jewish people, especially their youth, to the advent of Alexandrian imperialism was probably followed by a similar attraction to the new philosophy that it inspired, the philosophy of Stoicism, conceived by a Phoenician philosopher, a Semite, and evidently equally kindled by Alexander's cosmopolitan project. Scholars have always been puzzled by the incursion into the last chapters of the Book of Job of a new character, a young man, Elihu, the son of Barachel the Buzite. As we shall see, he was a spokesman for the new Phoenician philosophy whose Alexandrian and cosmopolitan pantheism attracted many young militants. That Elihu interrupted Job and his three comforters was symbolic of the manners of the new philosophers. By contrast, the Pharisees, as Josephus wrote, were respectful of "such as are advanced in years," nor so bold as to contradict them in anything which they have introduced."[10] Elihu, on the contrary, a proto-Sadducee, challenges forthrightly both Job's pessimism, on the one hand, and the complacent optimistic theism of his friends, on the other. Elihu speaks with the tone of the generational philosophic rebel:

> I am young, and ye are very old; Wherefore I held back . . . I said: "Days should speak, And multitude of years should teach wisdom!" But it is a spirit in man, and the breath of the Almighty that giveth them understanding. It is not the great that are wise, nor the aged that discern judgment. (32:6, 7, 8, 9)

It is noteworthy, however, that the term *Stoic,* unlike the word *Epicurean,* never became one of opprobrium in Talmudical literature. For *Epicurean* came to signify atheist disbelief and immoral living. Not so, however, with *Stoic,* whose philosophy and ethics were well-suited to blend with the outlook of young Jewish intellectuals who wished to articulate a higher idealistic spirit.

How, then, did this new Phoenician philosophy arise and spread in the eastern Mediterranean world? As William Foxwell Albright, the famed Johns Hopkins archaeologist and scholar, noted, "a rich Phoenician color" permeates the Book of Job: "Job and Ecclesiastes are both so full of Phoenician language, economic practice, cosmology, astronomy, and imagery that it is difficult to believe that either was written outside of the Phoenician sphere of higher culture." Albright, however, detected no sign of "Greek philosophical influence" in either Job or Ecclesiastes, and unlike most other scholars, he dated Job as not later than the mid-seventh century B.C.E.[11] In the opinion of other scholars, however, the Book of Job was written in the period before and during the fourth century B.C.E. The latter date would be especially consonant with the role of Elihu in completing what became a pentalogue, together with God's own magisterial reply, both expressing the impact of the rising new Phoenician—Hellenic Stoic philosophy.[12]

The knowledge of the Greek language and philosophy among Jewish scholars in Palestine had indeed become widespread by the time Ptolemy Philadelphus succeeded to the throne of Egypt in 285 B.C.E. That we can infer from the famed *Letter of Aristeas*, written about 270 B.C.E., describing how seventy-two Jewish scholars were brought to Alexandria to translate the Pentateuch from Hebrew into Greek: "They had not only acquired proficiency in the literature of the Jews, but had bestowed no slight study on that of the Greeks also." The Jews, said Aristeas, "eagerly seek intercourse with other nations, and they pay special care to this, and emulate each other therein." And in their dialogues with the king on wisdom, it was Stoic virtues, such as equanimity and courage, expressed in Stoic vocabulary, combined with a Stoic idea of a God who "in his Sovereignty consummates and guides the actions of us all," that came readily to their speech.[13]

Alexander the Great died in 323 B.C.E. Twelve years earlier, around 335 B.C.E., the founder of Stoicism, Zeno of Citium (Cyprus), was born. The city in which he lived was "partly occupied by Phoenician settlers," and Zeno, himself "of a dark complexion," was always identified with them. Crates, his teacher, called him "my little Phoenician," while another, Polemo, said to him: "you . . . steal my doctrines and then clothe them in Phoenician dress."[14] In the Phoenician towns of Tyre and Sidon, pupils of Zeno flourished, such as a namesake Zeno as well as Antipater who wrote a book on Zeno's doctrine. "That Zeno himself was a Phoenician is implied, I think, in all our records," wrote Edwyn Bevan. Moreover, a dynasty of Phoenician kings "whose names figure in the Punic inscriptions found on the spot" ruled Citium.[15] The "Citianeans of Sidon" also claimed Zeno as their countryman. He was, we might say, the representative Phoenician philosopher of this immediate era after Alexander's death.[16] Also, like many Phoenicians, he was the son of a merchant, and a merchant himself; indeed, according to Plutarch, Zeno turned to the life of a professional philosopher only when he learned that his one remaining merchant ship had been sunk at sea with all its cargo. "Much obliged, Fortune! You also drive me to the philosopher's cloak."[17] In effect, Elihu's advice to Job was to adopt a tempered form of this Zenonian Stoicism.

Phoenicia's coastal towns were places where Hebrew, Greek, and Phoenician merchants commingled in the marketplace as buyers and sellers. Hebrew merchants, according to the vivid economic reportage of the prophet Ezekiel, traded their wheat, honey, oil, and balm. The Greeks (Ionians) dealt in "the persons of men and vessels of brass," and together with the Dannites, went to the fairs to deal in "bright iron, cassia, and calamins." Despite the prophet Isaiah's animus against bourgeois traders, and his sombre forecast that Tyre, in its pursuit of profit, would "commit fornication with all the kingdoms of the world," he also acknowledged that the Phoenician entrepot was "the crowning city, whose merchants are princes, whose traffickers are the honorable of the earth" (Isaiah 23:8). In the Phoenician commercial towns, a competitive marketplace for ideas followed in the wake of the competitive market for goods. Citium, the birthplace of Zeno, called in the Hebrew Scripture "the land of Chittim" was one such partner in the interchange of ideas. Zeno proceeded from Citium to Athens around 312 B.C.E., and founded his school in 301 B.C.E.; winning renown within a year, the school's disciples were called Stoics because the teaching of Zeno took place in the Stoa (Colonnade, or Porch).

Stoicism, as Norman Bentwich wrote, thus emerged originally as a cosmopolitan philosophy conceived by "Hellenized Semites" who indeed, in his opinion, "borrowed much from Semitic sources."[18] Inspired by the cosmopolitan aspiration of Alexander's imperialism, Zeno wrote his famed book *The Republic,* the reply of Phoenician-born Stoicism to Plato's work by the same title. The book did not survive the sieve of the barbarian invasions, medieval Christianity, and the burning of the library at Alexandria,[19] but according to Plutarch, its teaching "may be summed up in this one main principle: that all the inhabitants of this world of ours should not live differentiated by their respective rules of justice into separate cities and communities, but that we should consider all men to be of one community and one polity, and that we should have a common life and an order common to us all, even as a herd that feeds together and shares the pasturage of a common field." As Plutarch stated it clearly, Zeno's philosophy was the intellectual heritage of Alexander's noble-minded imperialism: "This Zeno wrote, giving shape to a dream or, as it were, shadowy picture of a well-ordered and philosophic commonwealth; but it was Alexander who gave effect to the idea. For Alexander did not follow Aristotle's advice to treat the Greeks as if he were their leader, and other peoples as if he were their master; . . . for to do so would have been to cumber his leadership with numerous battles and banishments and festering seditions. But, as he believed that he came as a heaven-sent governor to all, and as a mediator for the whole world, . . . and he brought together in one great loving-cup, as it were, men's lives; . . . He bade them all consider as their fatherland the whole inhabited earth; . . ."[20]

Corresponding to the rational world-republic, Zeno and his Stoics proposed a rational, cosmic monotheism; a rational spirit indeed, pervaded all existence. They held that "God is a living being, immortal, rational, perfect, and intellectual in his happiness, unsusceptible of any kind of end. . . . He is the creator of the universe, and as it were, the father of all things in common. A portion of him pervades everything, . . . he pervades life." Beginning with Zeno, they said "the soul is a warm spirit; by it we have our breath, and by it we are moved."[21] A rationalistic outlook characterized Stoic thinking in all fields, from politics to physics. "The whole of the Stoic Physics," Edwyn Bevan commented, "was directed in showing that the Power operative in the Universe was rational."[22] God, according to Zeno and his disciples, was "the maker of the arrangement and order that we see." As the new philosophy spread through the eastern Mediterranean countries, reinforced by the growing eminence of the Stoic school, young Jewish thinkers, animated as young Phoenicians and Athenians were, by the daring Alexandrian cosmopolitan rationalism would have joined in the address to Zeno by the Greek Stoic Zenodotus, who compared him to Cadmus, the mythic prince of Phoenicia, who was reputed to have brought the alphabet to the Greeks:

> You taught a manly doctrine, and did found
> By your deep wisdom a great novel school,
> Chaste parent of unfearing liberty
> And if your country was Phoenicia
> Why need we grieve; from that land Cadmus came
> Who gave to Greece her written books of wisdom.[23]

Elihu, son of Barachel, was evidently filled with confidence in the new philosophy of the young intellectuals, this heady new Stoic philosophy. In its early phase, the doctrine could even take on a left revolutionary direction, as it did with the Stoic philosopher Sphaerus, the pupil of Zeno, who gave philosophic direction to the attempts by the young king, Cleomenes (235-219 B.C.E.), to restore communistic society to Sparta, an idealistic episode beautifully evoked in the novel by Naomi Mitchison *The Corn King and the Spring Queen*. The Stoic philosopher Blossius taught the Roman brothers Gracchi the principles underlying their struggle for agrarian democracy.[24] Elihu, son of Barachel, also regarded himself as an egalitarian: "For I know not to give flattering titles; . . ." (32:22). His message however, was one of Stoic rational theology, not of politics. Like the early Stoics, Elihu holds:

> The spirit of God hath made me,
> And the breath of the Almighty gave me life. (33:4)

Young Elihu, however, in accordance with the Stoic theology, ("He has not the figure of a man") has repudiated the features of the traditional anthropomorphism of the Mosaic creed; his is not the God whose back quarters Moses was privileged to see. He has no human features, and he rules Nature inscrutably; his ends and means are incommensurable with man's puny intelligence.

Though Elihu sometimes lapses into the standpoint of Job's three friends, he basically rejects their idea that Job's misery was inflicted upon him by God as a just punishment for sins that Job has committed but refuses to acknowledge. Rather, Elihu's conception is that of the Stoics, that there is a Reason in God's deeds that transcends the human understanding; somehow the evils we experience play their part in the divine pattern; Job's miseries were not, therefore, punishments decreed by a Divine Judge but rather necessary incidents in the divine scheme of things. That the phenomena and laws of God's physical and biological universes are marvelously beyond the scale of human comprehension attests to the transcendence of God's Reason over feeble human reason. And if God's Reason is so patently powerful, though not intelligible to us, may we not extrapolate and affirm that Job's suffering also has its place and explanation in the Unknowable Reason?

Zeno and his Stoic disciples had envisaged a God whose "mind penetrates into every part of the world, just as the soul pervades us," and who rules this "one" world by universal laws that determine its "creation and destruction."[25] Zeno's lost book *On the Universe* had outlined this cosmological outlook, even proposing explanations for the eclipses of the sun and the moon. His modern counterpart in the twentieth century, the famous H. G. Wells, likewise seemed to derive or associate his ideas of a socialistic world state from or with the laws of biological evolution. Similarly, Zeno's world-republic seemed a corollary of the activities of God the Natural Scientist. Therefore Elihu also reminds Job and his friends of God's natural creations that are beyond human comprehension: "Behold, God is great, beyond our knowledge; . . . For He draweth away the drops of water, . . . Which the skies pour down, And drop upon the multitudes of men. Yea, can any understand the spreading of the clouds, . . . He sendeth it forth under the whole heaven, and His lightning unto the ends of the earth . . . He thundereth with the voice of His majesty; . . . Great things doeth he, which we cannot comprehend. . . .Dost thou know the balancings of the clouds, The wondrous works of him who is perfect in knowledge?" (36:26, 27, 28; 37:3, 5, 16). And then, almost as an afterthought about humans, or possibly through an editorial insertion, the poetry of God the Physical and Natural Scientist is followed by a solitary, unconvincing statement of God as Social Scientist: "The Almighty, whom we cannot find out, is excellent in power, yet to judgment, and plenteous justice He doeth no violence" (37:23).

Elihu's philosophy of God the Rational Naturalist is that indeed which God Himself adopts in His own supreme answer to Job. God invokes His role "when I laid the foundations of the earth," and "the morning stars sang together" (38:47). The snow, the rains, the clouds, the springs of the sea, and in the skies, the Pleiades and the bands of Orion, all attest His wisdom. The world of living things—the goats, the peacocks, ostriches, horses, grasshoppers, hawks, and eagles, possibly the hippopotami, and the mysterious leviathan—all are catalogued in the argument for God's Power, but of the world of the melancholy chronicles of human suffering, He ventures not more than the affirmation that "he is a king over all the children of pride." "Behold, I answer thee," Elihu had said, "that God is too great for man, . . . He shall breaketh in pieces mighty men without inquisition, . . . and He heareth the cry of the afflicted . . . and when He hideth his face, who then can behold Him? Whether it be done unto a nation or unto a man alike . . ." (33:12; 34:24, 28, 29).

The Hebraic reception of Stoicism, however, was not unqualified; where Zeno's doctrines came afoul of the Hebraic cultural mores and the biblical personal ethic, they were repudiated. Elihu, the son of Barachel, stands together with Job, for instance, in refusing to consider the Stoic recourse to suicide as a way out of insoluble problems. As Eduard Zeller noted,[26] Zeno of Citium had died a voluntary death, as did his successor Cleanthes of Assus, remembered for his eloquent monotheistic hymn to Zeus. Cleanthes, when he reached Zeno's age, died from voluntary starvation. The next successor to the headship of the Stoa, Chrysippus also committed suicide.[27] Elihu, however, for all his enthusiasm for the Stoic theology, never challenges Job's resolve to live. Job may curse the day he was born but he will not draw the pragmatic consequence of suicide in an apparently hopeless situation. It will be up to God to slay him, but he will not choose to do so himself. The Book of Job is the Bible's closest approach to a discussion of suicide, and its greatest influence on ethics perhaps derives precisely from its rejection of the Greco-Roman acceptance of suicide. Perhaps the survival of the Jews has owed something to this Joban mandate. And the Book of Job's ethic of survival has been at least as influential as its agnostic rationalism concerning the consistency of the evils of human existence with the attributes or existence of God.

Zeno and his disciples, the "new philosophers" in Athens, had, moreover, a kind of youthful intellectual bravado about experimenting intellectually with the last conceivable consequence of their doctrine. Zeno advocated sexual communism, or promiscuity, as well as the economic variety, again very much as H. G. Wells did later. "They also teach that women ought to be in common among the wise, so that whoever meets with any may enjoy her," wrote Diogenes Laertius.[28] They argued that such a practice would make all children equally loved. It does not seem to have occurred to Zeno and Chrysippus that it was far more likely that all children would be equally unloved. In any case, this Stoic doctrine could find no foothold where the Hebraic institution of the family was strong. And Zeno's social dream was also darkened with a social nightmare when a Stoic disciple counseled to "even eat human meat if there should be occasion."[24] Elihu, the son of Barachel, would not have repealed "the covenant of Noah" that was binding upon non-Jews as well. On the other hand, the Stoic philosophy brought an emphasis on the value of friendship that had been hitherto virtually ignored in the Hebrew writings, except for the extraordinary case of David and Jonathan. "And they describe friendship itself as communion of life," wrote Diogenes Laertius, and "say that friendship exists in the virtuous alone." Whatever their differences it was a landmark for Hebrew experience that the four friends Job, Bildad, Eliphaz, and Zophar spent more than a week together in mourning and argument.[29] One wishes one knew how they had met, for all came from different places.

Evidently the new philosophy of Elihu struck the orthodox Palestinian Jews of around 100 B.C.E. as heretical. For in the pseudepigraphic Testament of Job that was written at that time, Elihu is depicted as "filled with Satan" and uttering "arrogant words" against Job for which he is then "censured" by the Lord, who refuses to accept him as "worthy" of offering sacrifices. Job's friend Eliphaz also characterizes Elihu as "the only wicked one," one of "darkness and not of light," who "will have no memorial among the living." Job himself admonishes his sons: "Do not take wives for yourselves from foreigners"; alien indoctrinations were feared. And there seems to be a gloating reference to the decline of the Alexandrian imperialism that was the political expression of the new philosophy that Elihu advocated: "His kingdom has passed away, his throne has decayed, and the honor of (his) pretense is in hades."[30]

Though the narrative opening and conclusion of Job were probably written some centuries before the Hebraic Stoic additions of Elihu and God's address, and the dialogues of Job and his three friends were probably composed during the intervening period, the entry of Elihu marked the first welcome contact of Hebraic thought with the new humanism that Zeno the Phoenician formulated in the Alexandrian era. However, the Hebraic form of Stoicism clung more closely to the idea of a personal God than did the founder of Stoicism, whose doctrine always verged on a pantheism. The pantheist creed tended to require that personal suffering should be endured as part of the necessary workings of the Impersonal Reason, and the Stoic recipe for happiness would make a man independent of the fluctuations of fortune by having him his identify his will with God's Impersonal Reason. Even the agonies of torture and disease could be surmounted, in the Stoic view, by "internalizing" their occurrence, and making them consonant with our will. To such reasoning, Job remains impervious to the end. He will engage in no effort at the transmutation of evil into good through some psychological chemistry or self-hypnotism. So long as the hypothesis of God's existence retains some minimal probability, he will maintain his faith and contribute all the more energetically to fulfill its moral intent. And in so doing, he avoids recasting the evil in pain into an instrument for the perverse pleasure of self-hatred. From a metaphysical standpoint, he remains an agnostic, thus sharing the outlook of Ecclesiastes in a common wisdom. For a metaphysical agnosticism has always been part of the wisdom standpoint. The "lesson," the principal object of the whole Book of Job, as the wise Maimonides wrote in his *Guide for the Perplexed* in the thirteenth century, was that "we are unable to comprehend the nature of God's creation and conduct of things." Or as Charles Darwin put it, the doubt cannot be dispelled, and "always arises whether the convictions of man's mind, which has been developed from the mind of the lower animals, are of any value or at all trustworthy."[31]

The promise of Stoicism as a cosmopolitan, humanist philosophy was to a considerable extent fulfilled during the first centuries of the Roman Empire.[32] Meanwhile, too, Stoic professional philosophers also acquired a full measure of the traits not infrequently associated with the professional guild, "empty boasting" and compulsive contrariety, and were expelled from Rome under Vespasian. For all philosophical and political movements are also governed by laws of rise and decline, and every philosophical idea is therefore multi-potential in its practical applications. Stoicism, that had been founded under Semitic auspices, actually later provided the doctrinal basis for the most virulent anti-Semitic agitation in the Middle East. Job, Elihu, and Job's three friends would have been astounded. For such Stoic anti-Semites as Apion and Chaeremon waged an effective campaign against the Jews, regarding them as their chief religious and political rivals.[33] One is reminded of the analogous career of Soviet materialism as an ideology; though at its beginning Lenin praised the Jews for their disproportionately large contribution to the revolutionary ranks, and scorned anti-Semitism, Stalin managed to convert their Marxist doctrine into an ideological basis for anti-Semitism, and largely succeeded in his not unpopular policy of expelling Jewish intellectuals from Soviet politics. And if Cleanthes, a successor to Zeno's headship of the Stoa, declared that Aristarchus, originator of the heliocentric hypothesis and forerunner of Copernicus, should be indicted for impiety,[34] students of Einstein's theory of relativity fared likewise in the Soviet Union, where they were long persecuted as anti-dialectical and anti-materialist.[35]

Curiously, the Book of Job has been ignored by such philosophers as Nietzsche and Schopenhauer. The reason, I think, is not far to seek. Both of them as atheists would have regarded Job's persistent belief in God as unwarranted, as an *idée fixe*. But in that case, would they have had any argument for keeping Job from committing suicide? Both German philosophers repudiated suicide on grounds that from Elihu's standpoint were dubious; why should Nietzsche, pathetically on the verge of life-long insanity, have clung to living unless strengthened to do so by an uneliminable belief in an underlying divine ingredient in the universe? And one would have thought that Schopenhauer, if he genuinely believed his doctrine, would have resolved to outwit the treacherous will-to-live and its perpetual treadmill of individual existence by terminating it. Did he refuse to slay himself for the same reasons that affected Job?

On the other hand, Thomas Hobbes, the most militant polemicist and excrementalist in the history of philosophy—that is, its most frequent user of excremental epithet and metaphor—welcomed the Book of Job for confirming his own authoritarian (possibly totalitarian) view that "power irresistible justifies all actions really and properly."[36] For Hobbes, God's argument: "Where wert thou when I laid the foundations of the earth?" is no example of the fallacious *argumentum ad baculum* (the appeal to superior force) but rather the major premise of all political ethics. Hobbes, however, seems to have misread the Book of Job; for Elihu appeals not to God's sheer power but rather to the proposition that since such power had been used to fashion so wondrous a nature, then doubtless it was great and intelligent enough to provide a solution equally wondrous for the role of suffering in the world. Undeniably a leap of faith is blended with this reasoning, for the terms of that solution to the equation for the unknown value of evil is not given to men but only to God. Hobbes's formula is, in effect, a psychological resolution to identify himself with God's power, even when by human standards, it is evil. Hobbes had a remarkable readiness to accept unflinchingly whatever paradoxical consequences followed from his axioms. Thus, having defined all existents as necessarily corporeal, he calmly assented to the consequence that all mental events were "phantasms," and God was corporeal.

Immanuel Kant, on the other hand, found that Job was a Kantian hero; the Book of Job, in his view, conveyed the lesson that "all further attempts of 'human wisdom' to fathom the ways of divine wisdom must be abandoned." What God held against Job's friends, what angered Him, was that they pretended to have answers that they did not have; "they affirmed things of which they should have confessed they had no knowledge and with which they feigned convictions which in fact they did not have." On the other hand, according to Kant, God was pleased with "Job's free and sincere outspokenness;" Job spoke "in good faith," and it was not the merit or his "insight" but "only the uprightness of the heart" that constituted Job's greatness; that was why God preferred him to the pious flatterers.[37] According to Kant, Job did not base his morality upon his faith, but his faith upon his morality; however weak that faith was, it was "a truer and purer one" than it would be in a religion based on self-interest.

There was, however, no reason for Kant to impugn the sincerity of Job's friends. They had come from afar to mourn with him when all others deserted him. Their tears of mourning for seven days were shed in sincere grief for their friend Job. And if they tried to find a meaning of retribution in his suffering, perhaps by the same token they were reaching for a redemption that would follow upon the misery. For they believed in a just God completely. Then, too, perhaps the rumor had reached them that Job, in fulfilling his judicial duties, had shown a growing contempt toward some pathetic pleaders who appeared before him. Were Job's friends wrong to walk slowly before they abandoned their belief that God was just? Has any primitive or pre-industrial society survived that professed an atheist alternative? Or would the hostility of a godless world have finally overwhelmed the primitive mind?

What Kant perhaps overlooks, however, is that Job's sincerity rests on the fact that he does not abandon, or repress, the search for some intellectual answer to the "problem of evil." If that search "to fathom the ways of divine wisdom" were entirely repressed, as Kant counsels, then the religious faith that is founded on not more than a provisional, intellectual answer to ultimate issues would tend to wither, to become hollow. Job does not base his faith solely on the need for a basis to his morality, but rather on the conviction that this morality partakes of the underlying rationality of the universe, that a rational universe is necessarily a moral one. Let us grant that the arguments of Elihu and the Stoics for the existence of a rational, moral God are slender in their force, for they argue from a sample drawn from physical laws to a faith in a corresponding rationality in sociological law as well as perhaps in a psychological transcendence to possibly a human immortality. In the human sciences, however, there have been no Einsteins, no Eddingtons, to make us marvel at the rationality and elegance of sociological law; Freud could not take pride in man, and Marx and Engels made hatred the dynamic of history. Nonetheless, the spokesmen for the wisdom tradition, from Michel Montaigne to Benjamin Franklin to William James, have seen no better foundation for their philosophy than this Joban-Stoic argument of slender force. Gottfried W. Leibniz, struggling powerfully with this problem, although refraining strangely from engaging the arguments of the Book of Job, maintained that life as a whole was more pleasurable than painful,[38] and occasionally, statistical studies have been adduced to support his view. We would answer that if a representative sample of humanity were questioned, seeking out all types of societies; and if to that sample were added what we know of past societies; and if, lastly, our questionings took sufficient account of those who had traversed all the ages of life, it is doubtful that life's experience in its purely earthly career would arouse much enthusiasm. One can understand why William James felt that the enterprise of life might capitulate to a suicidal choice unless sustained by at least a slender theistic leap.

NOTES

1. Martin L. Diamond, *Martin Buber: Jewish Existentialist,* New York, 1960, pp. 209-210.

2. *The Babylonian Talmud, Baba Bathra,* tr. Maurice Simon, ed. I. Epstein, London, 1935, pp. 75-80.

3. Nahum M. Sarna, "Bible," *Encyclopaedia Judaica,* Vol. 4, Jerusalem, 1971, p. 824.

4. Job 25:4.

5. Samuel I. Mintz, *The Hunting of Leviathan: Seventeenth-Century Reactions to the Materialism and Moral Philosophy of Thomas Hobbes,* Cambridge, England, 1962, p. 122.

6. Job, 23:3; 31:35.

7. Louis Finkelstein, *The Pharisees: The Sociological Background of their Faith,* 2 vols., Philadelphia, 1938, Vol. I, pp. 230-233.

8. Robert Gordis, "The Social Background of Wisdom Literature," *Hebrew Union College Annual* 18 (1944): 113-114. Robert Gordis, *The Book of God and Man: A Study of Job,* Chicago, 1965, rept., 1968, pp. 50-52.

9. Flavius Josephus, *The Works, Antiquities of the Jews,* Book XI, Chapter VIII, Section 5, tr. William Whiston, Philadelphia, 1872, p. 338. George Sarton speaks "of the cardinal fact that the Alexandrian Renaissance was a complete renaissance." The first two Ptolemies "mainly accomplished" that Renaissance: the Museum and the Library were founded at which such scientists as Euclid and Aristarchus, Hipparchus and Eratosthenes did their work, and the Bible was translated into Greek. *Ancient Science and Modern Civilization,* Lincoln 1954, p. 6.

10. Norman Bentwich, *Philo-Judaeus of Alexandria,* Philadelphia, 1910, rept. 1948, p. 64. Flavius Josephus, *The Works, Antiquities of the Jews,* Book X, Chapter XI, Section 7, p. 358.

11. William Foxwell Albright, *Yahweh and the Gods of Canaan: A Historical Analysis of Two Contrasting Faiths,* New York, 1969, p. 260.

12. See Louis Finkelstein, op. cit. Vol. I, p. 231. Morris Jastrow, Jr., *The Book of Job,* Philadelphia, 1920, p. 36. Robert Gordis, *The Book of God and Man,* p. 216. "While the completed book may be as late as the third century B.C.," writes Marvin H. Pope, "it may also be several centuries earlier." *Job,* Anchor Bible, 3d ed., New York, 1979, p. XL.

13. Moses Hadas, tr., ed., *Aristeas to Philocrates (Letter of Aristeas),* 1951, rept., New York, 1973, pp. 149, 177-179. Also, pp. 186, 187, 194, 195, 196, 201. Bentwich, *Philo-Judaeus of Alexandria,* p. 32.

14. Diogenes Laertius, *The Lives and Opinions of Eminent Philosophers,* tr. C. D. Yonge, London, rept. 1895, pp. 259-268; revised, in Moses Hadas, ed., *Essential Works of Stoicism,* New York, 1967, pp. 1-10.

15. Edwyn Bevan, *Stoics and Sceptics,* Oxford, 1913, pp. 14-15.

16. "A group of shrewd Semitic families domiciled in Citium, and doing business round the shores of the Levant—such was the milieu whence Zeno came in his youth to fourth-century Athens." Edwyn Bevan, *Stoics and Sceptics,* p. 15.

17. *Plutarch's Moralia,* tr. W. C. Humbold, Cambridge, Massachusetts, 1939, Vol. VI, p. 183. "[H]is contemporaries thought of him [Zeno] as a Phoenician." Moses Hadas, *Hellenistic Culture: Fusion and Diffusion,* New York, 1959, p. 106.

18. Norman Bentwich, *Philo-Judaeus of Alexandria,* p. 64.

19. George Sarton, *Ancient Science and Modern Civilization,* Lincoln, Nebraska, 1954, p. 13.

20. *Plutarch's Moralia,* Vol. IV, tr. Frank Cole Babbitt, Cambridge, Massachusetts, 1936, pp. 397-399. Also see W. W. Tarn, *Alexander the Great,* Cambridge, England, Vol. I, 1948, p. 147. Vol. II, p. 417ff. Aristotle wrote in his *Politics:* "The Hellenic race . . . if it could be formed into one state, would be able to rule the world." See Hans Kelsen, "The Philosophy of Aristotle and the Hellenic-Macedonian Policy," *The International Journal of Ethics* 48 (1937): 60.

21. Diogenes Laertius, op. cit., pp. 312, 317. Moses Hadas, *Essential Works of Stoicism,* pp. 34, 46.

22. Edwyn Bevan, *Stoics and Sceptics,* p. 40.

23. Hadas, *Essential Works of Stoicism,* pp. 40, 12.

24. Plutarch, *The Lives of the Noble Grecians and Romans,* tr. John Dryden, rev. Arthur Hugh Clough, rept., New York, 1932, pp. 973, 998. D. R. Dudley, "Blossius of Cumae," *The Journal of Roman Studies* 31 (1942): 98. Lewis Feuer, *Imperialism and the Anti-Imperialist Mind,* New York, 1986, p. 14.

25. Hadas, *Essential Works of Stoicism,* pp. 36, 40, 41, 43.

26. Eduard Zeller, *Outlines of the History of Greek Philosophy,* tr. L. R. Palmer, New York, 1931, p. 209. Hadas, *Essential Works of Stoicism,* p. 38. In Diogenes Laertius' words: "And they say that a wise man will very rationally take himself out of life, either for the sake of his country or of his friends, or if he is in bitter pain, or under the affliction of mutilation, or incurable diseases."

27. R. D. Hicks, *Stoic and Epicurean,* New York, 1910, rept., 1961, p. 7.

28. Hadas, *Essential Works of Stoicism,* p. 38.

29. Diogenes Laertius, op. cit., pp. 303, 309, 311, Hadas, *Essential Works of Stoicism,* p. 35.

30. Robert A. Kraft, ed., *The Testament of Job,* Missoula, Montana, 1974, pp. 71, 75, 77, 79.

31. "Letter of Charles Darwin to W. Graham, July 3, 1881," in Sir Francis Darwin, ed. *Autobiography of Charles Darwin,* London, 1929, p. 153. Idem., p. 149.

32. See. Miriam T. Griffin, *Seneca: A Philosopher in Politics,* Oxford, 1976, A. N. Sherwin-White, *Racial Prejudice in Imperial Rome,* Cambridge, England, 1967, pp. 82-83.

33. Norman Bentwich, *Philo-Judaeus of Alexandria,* p. 63. Flavius Josephus, *The Works, Against Apion,* Book II, Sections 13, 21, pp. 509, 514. Norman Bentwich, *Josephus,* Philadelphia, 1914, pp. 236-207.

34. William H. Stahl, "Aristarchus of Samos," *Dictionary of Scientific Biography,* New York, 1970, Vol. I, p. 248. J. B. Bury et al., *The Hellenistic Age,* 1923, rept., New York, 1970, pp. 16-17. Thomas W. Africa, "Copernicus' Relation to Aristarchus and Pythagoras," *Isis,* 1961, Vol. 52, pp. 406-407. Ludwig Edelstein, *The Meaning*

of Stoicism, Cambridge, Massachusetts, 1966, p. 30. Edwyn Bevan, *A History of Egypt under the Ptolemaic Dynasty,* London, 1927, pp. 124-126.

35. See my *Einstein and the Generations of Science,* 1974, 2d ed. New Brunswick, 1982, pp. 29, 46, 96.

36. Sir William Molesworth, ed., *The English Works of Thomas Hobbes of Malmesbury,* London, 1839-45, Vol. IV, p. 250.

37. Immanuel Kant, "On the Failure of all Attempted Philosophical Theodicies," translated in Michel Despland, *Kant on History and Religion,* Montreal, 1973, pp. 290-293. Also, see A. L. Loades, *Kant and Job's Comforters,* Newcastle Upon Tyne, England, 1985, p. 42.

38. Gottfried Wilhelm Leibniz, *Theodicy,* ed., Diogenes Allen, tr. E. M. Huggard, p. 131.

8

Building a Biblical Foundation
for Contemporary Ethics

Ellis Rivkin

At the outset, I should like to stress the fact that the Bible was centuries
in the making and consists of a diversity of books written at different
times for different purposes, by a wide variety of individuals impelled
by a wide variety of interests. Many of the books of the Bible gave
compelling evidence that they were not written by a single hand. The
five books of Moses, for example, are so completely multi-layered that
scholars are still seeking to unravel their intricate webbing. To speak
then of biblical ethics as though it were a body of agreed upon principles
is to speak of a body of ethics that is nowhere to be found in the Bible.
Only if biblical ethics is taken to be that record of the variety of ethical
responses to changing problems that prophets, priests, kings, and other
Israelite leaders came up with in the course of the historical experience
of Israel can we juxtapose biblical ethics to contemporary ethics.

When we do make such a juxtaposition, we discover that though
the conceptual frameworks may radically differ, the process by which
ethical principles are established turn out to be very much the same.
In the biblical world, as in our own, human beings grappled with internal
and external realities that were only partially understood; sought to
comprehend them as best they could with the conceptual tools at hand;
came up with now this now that judgment as to how they might best
be handled; and did not hold back from modifying, or even discarding,

Ellis Rivkin is Adolph S. Ochs Professor of Jewish History at the Hebrew
Union College-Jewish Institute of Religion.

judgments previously made, or from making quantum leaps into as yet unexplored realms of ethical possibility. Although "Thus saith the Lord" may, on first reading, seem to resonate with an almighty absolutism, this absolutism fades away as one goes from one "Thus saith the Lord" to another.

When, however, one dissolves the framework of Yahwistic absolutism, one discovers that biblical ethics is neither more nor less relative, neither more nor less compelling, than the ethics that has emerged within the framework of critical reason.

The biblical framework does indeed presuppose an omnipotent and omniscient God, but the stuff that is found therein testifies to a God who has continuously given his assent, if not his mandate, to whatever time and tide demand. Every major structural stage was given its distinctive imprimatur: patriarchal, prophetic, monarchical, and hierarchical. Every significant historical event was stamped, as a matter of course, with divine confirmation: enslavement, wilderness wandering, conquest, settlement, imperial ravaging, exile, restoration, and Persian hegemony. Every prophet's oracle was fitted to the occasion, and not subjected to a repetitive formula. There were in fact times when one did not know from moment to moment what God's will might be, and there were other times when God seemed to be speaking in a cacophony of prophetic voices demanding both this and that, both right and left, both yea and nay. When the Bible is liberated from the forbidding framework of divine absolutism and then read, it reveals a God who is responsive to the vicissitudes of history, open to the implications of change, and supportive of the quest for ethical and moral principles without dogmatic precommitment to any previous revelation. The God of Israel thus shows himself in the biblical record to have been seen as an ever-changing God whose will today could not be counted on to be his will on the morrow. As a consequence, biblical ethics emerges as a mosaic of insets configured by a problem-solving people bound in covenant to a problem-solving God.

The insets of this mosaic are not difficult to extricate from the biblical record so that the ethical components of each can be seen and evaluated independently. Thus when we look at the patriarchal inset, we are struck by the deep appreciation of the patriarchs for the willingness of the settled people among whom they sojourned to allow them to move freely throughout the land, and by their wish to reciprocate in such a manner as to earn the approbation of their gracious hosts. Indeed this memory of abiding hospitality became so sharply etched in the minds of the people of Israel that it came to be woven into the warp and woof of the people's concept of its highest self as a people duty-bound to cherish and love the stranger.

The patriarchs also seem to have placed a high value on hospitality to unexpected guests; to settling quarrels peacefully; to respecting the mores of peoples who allowed them to sojourn in the land, even when this respect, on occasion, required dissembling; and on societies free of licentiousness, corruption, and base dealing. Reflective of a semi-nomadic mode of life, patriarchal ethics generated and sustained some values worthy, it would seem, of readaptation in our contemporary world.

The ethics that emerged from enslavement to Pharoah and from the wilderness wanderings likewise have a contemporaneous appeal. Slavery is pictured as unjust, cruelty as reprehensible, and freedom as good. At the same time, forgiveness for past wrongs and mistreatment is held to be a good. The Egyptians are neither to be abhorred nor barred entry into the congregation of the Lord.

The ethics we can glean from the first two stages of Israel's history are not, however, free of what we might now consider flaws. Concubinage was not frowned upon and the casting out of a concubine's son is condoned. Tit for tat is not condemned; deception in a good and worthy cause is not disallowed; and the absolute authority of the leader and of the leader's God is rarely challenged.

With the conquest of the land and its settlement, however, the ethical values of the people look a sharp and harsh turn. Whereas the patriarchs were sojourners in a land freely acknowledged as not belonging to them, Joshua was bent on wiping out the seven nations living in Canaan. He justified so total a conquest by conjuring up the will of a God who insisted that no mercy was to be shown. So, too, the prophet Samuel lashes out at Saul for not having heeded God's command to exterminate the Amalekits, stripping him of his crown for having disobeyed the divine will. The God of liberation from the taskmaster's whip was transmuted into a God who demanded the eradication of the seven nations, who dwelled in Canaan, and who withheld compassion for babe and suckling child whose misfortune it was to have been born to an Amalekite. In the heat of conquest, Israelite leaders forged an ethic justifying total war and gave it a divine hallmark—a hallmark that came to coexist alongside hallmarks no less bearing the imprimatur of a compassionate, loving, and forgiving God who cared for the stranger and the alien.

The ethic of total war achieved its goal. The Canaanites were thoroughly subjugated, even if they were not thoroughly annihilated. But this biblical ethic did not remain unchallenged. Confronted with both a society wallowing in corruption and the ravagings of imperial nations on the march, prophetic voices bespoke a far different God than that who had commanded the wiping out of the Canaanites and the other peoples living in the land. These prophets articulated an ethic so humane and so redolent with human hope and aspiration that it is hard even today to conceive a humanistic ethic that goes beyond the imperatives that logically follow from those insights proclaimed by Amos, Hosea, Micah, and Isaiahs I and II as being the very word of Yahweh.

Let us consider these insights that lead to an ethic of interpersonal relationships, an intersocietal ethic worthy of contemporary follow-through. These may be briefly summed up as the pursuit of equity and justice; the cultivation of loving kindness and compassion, as values to be given priority over economic, social, political, cultic, and institutional claims, and according to the individual a sacrosanct status vis-à-vis authoritarian nullification of these values. Did not Amos defy the Yahwistic authorities who denounced his values as threatening to Yahwistic establishmentarianism? And was it not Amos who affirmed his right to speak out in Yahweh's name, even though he was neither a prophet nor the son of a prophet but an individual bursting with intuitive insight?

These prophets were thus in effect affirming that there is a hierachy of values divinely implanted within the universe and that at the very summit of this hierarchy is the right of the individual to be treated justly and with compassion—and to speak out. At that time, "Thus saith the Lord" was the only means at hand by which Amos, Isaiah, and other prophets could give these values an ontological status capable of offsetting the ontological status being given to institutional and cultic values by other prophets who no less proclaimed "Thus saith the Lord."

These prophets in fact gave an ontological status to a whole array of human hopes and aspirations that they believed would be fulfilled in the fullness of time. They brushed aside empirical obstructions to their utopian assumptions as irrelevant. They believed god, not man, reigned over future possibilities. Thus Isaiah did not hesitate to proclaim that a day would come when Egypt, Assyria, and Israel would be equal in God's sight; when swords would be beaten into ploughshares and spears into pruning hooks; when the wolf would lie down with the lamb, and children would frolic over the den of the asp; when exploitation would be no more; and when death itself would die.

Prophetic anticipations such as these translate easily into any contemporary ethic aimed at motivating individuals to strive for a world beyond warring nations; for a human community rid of exploitation and repression; for cessation of war between human beings and nature. Today, as then, these hopes, ideals, and aspirations may prove to be vain, but this does not nullify their ethical value.

The ethical imperatives articulated by Amos, Hosea, Micah, and Isaiah—imperatives focusing as they did on interpersonal relations, societal infrastructure, international relations, and future possibilities— were themselves capped by a quantum leap that carried with it a first principle from which a biblical foundation of contemporary ethics can be deductively derived. This quantum leap was the first chapter of the book of Genesis.

Stripped of its time-bound form and mode of expression, the first chapter of Genesis gives us a single being the consequence of whose existence is a hierarchical universe that has at its apex a single individual, pictured as being the image of God, who is endowed by this creator-God with the right and the power to make of this universe what he or she wills. However omnipotent this God may appear to be, it is evident that this God does not have the power to deprive the individual of his or her free will, even when the individual defies God's commands and goes his or her own aberrant way.

This Being is pictured as having created a universe and not a particular land or a particular people. So, too, did He create a single individual and not a tribe, or a race, or a nation, or a class, or a gender. The first individual was created in this Being's image and often this Being's likeness—an image and likeness that was no more male than it was female—and this individual was given carte blanche to draw out either the good built into the universe or the evil that the rejection of the good would bring in its train. All of creation was thus made dependent on the human choice.

What are the ethical imperatives that follow logically from an affirmation that the outcome of the universe is dependent on the choices that the individual will make in his or her efforts to shape the universe in such a way as to fulfill ideal aspirations, whether they be good or evil, worthy or unworthy, possible or impossible in relationship to what the ultimate laws governing the universe allow?

Beginning as we must with the free-choosing individual, it would seem to follow necessarily that the preservation of that individual must be the ultimate concern of ethics. All other concerns must pale before this and assume the role of corollaries, not axioms. The questions that must be addressed are those that focus on how a universal infrastructure can be built that guarantees freedom and choice to individuals. A cornerstone of such an infrastructure will necessarily be the proviso that no individual, group, race, nation state, or ideology may remove this cornerstone. Since such a cornerstone has yet to be built, the critical ethical imperative on the agenda is its construction. And of all the obstacles that stand in the way of building this cornerstone is the division of the world into sovereign nation states that elevate national rights over the rights of the individual. Was it not the stirring up of national frenzy that made a shambles of Europe in World War I? Was it not an appeal to nationalism and racism that justified Hitler's ravagings of the European continent and the perpetration of an unprecendented Holocaust? Is it not an appeal to national rights that even now justifies the "hot" wars among third world nations, and the cold war between the superpowers? Until this critical problem is solved and the as yet unbuilt cornerstone is constructed, every individual will be haunted with the fear that his or her individuality may some day be ravaged. It thus turns out that the prime ethical imperative that follows from the first chapter of Genesis is the prime ethical imperative we need today: the building of a transnational world in which the right of the individual to choose freely is everywhere vouchsafed.

Here then is a biblical foundation on which a contemporary ethic may be built. It is not *the* biblical foundation. The Bible itself is a storehouse filled with foundations for whatever ethical system one might wish to build. It is the record of a people's odyssey with a God who was responsive to the tides of time, circumstance, and changing futures; a God for all seasons; a God whose omnipotence lay in his power to continuously become other than he was thought and proclaimed to have been. Yet by virtue of this proclivity for change, this God turns out to be but a mirror image of the reality that human beings have contended with and must still contend with when they seek ethical principles and certitudes. For like the God of Israel, reality is always changing, no less for contemporary minds searching with the tools of critical reason than for those minds of yesteryear who searched with the tools of intuitive insight and "naive" faith. How many times since the Copernican Revolution has the reality probed by the critical mind changed? How many mutually imcompatible ethical systems have been deduced from the Newtonian, the Darwinian, the Einsteinian, the Planckian models of reality? And what deductions will be made in the years to come? Should "strings" theory, the mathematics of chaos, and mind-imitating computers compel us to acknowledge that the reality we had come to take for granted was not as total as we thought it to be?

Israel's changing concept of God and our changing realities may thus not be so different despite the radically different presuppositions about God that may separate us from the biblical writers—except in one most important respect. Whereas the changing God of the Bible was enveloped by the dogmatic belief that he changed not at all; and whereas even the most audacious of the prophets ascribed their intuitive insights and mental ruminations to a direct revelation from God, contemporary thinkers are free of those dogmatic and doctrinal constraints that in the past sought to keep critical reason in check. The framework that bounds our quest for truth assures that the quest will be unbounded. It is this difference that makes all the difference in the world and it was for this reason that logical imperatives of the first chapter of Genesis were doomed to be overwhelmed by the logical disjunctions that coexist alongside them in the biblical canon, and by the overarching assumptions of a God external to the universe and humankind and endowed with the power to will and execute the impossible.

By contrast, the ethical imperatives drawn by contemporary thinkers can be spelled out with logical rigor in the hope that rational minds will see that if we begin with the free-choosing individual as the cornerstone of our ethic, and with a reality that is accessible to individual minds irrespective of the bodies in which they are housed, or the country in which they find themselves, then the ethical imperative that follows is the building of a global infrastructure supportive of the free-thinking and free-choosing individual who will be guided by ethical imperatives logically following from this enhanced stage of human possibility. On that day, but only on that day, will a biblical foundation of contemporary ethics become the foundation of a freely acknowledged universal ethic.

Part Two

Religious Ethics and Humanist Alternatives

9

The Relativity of Biblical Ethics

Joe Edward Barnhart

It is an axiom among fundamentalists and evangelicals that theology is the foundation of ethics and morality in North American culture. Without this foundation, they fear, ethics would fragment into total relativism or dissolve into whim, arbitrariness, and chaos. I would like to contest that view by showing how some organized religions are parasitical to the body of ethics and how the Bible itself exemplifies moral relativism.

Various theologians of the Middle Ages raised the interesting question of whether right and wrong are whatever God decrees them to be. For example, if God had commanded "Thou shall rape thrice daily," would it have been morally right to carry out the command and wrong to disobey it? If divine decree is not only the source but the *ultimate criterion* of right and wrong, is there any basis for trusting the Supreme Being who concocts the meaning of right and wrong? Indeed, were this putative Being to trick his creatures by scrambling the consequences of commands and prohibitions, it would be irrational to call Him evil; He is the Cosmic Existentialist who invents right and wrong *ex nihilo*. If He should lie, deceive, order Joshua to slaughter the Canaanites, or command rape, He could do all this and still label Himself as perfectly good.

Apparently having second thoughts about a Supreme Being un-restrained by moral principles, in the year of his death C. S. Lewis wrote: "The real danger is of coming to believe such dreadful things about Him. The conclusion I dread is not 'So there's no God after

---

Joe Edward Barnhart is professor of philosophy at North Texas State University.

all,' but 'So this is what God is really like. Deceive yourself no longer.'"[1] Only four months before his death, Lewis wrote in a letter to an American philosopher that there were dangers in judging God by moral standards. However, he maintained that "believing in a God whom we cannot but regard as evil, and then, in mere terrified flattery calling Him 'good' and worshipping Him, is still greater danger."[2] Lewis was responding specifically to the question of Joshua's slaughter of the Canaanites by divine decree and Peter's striking Ananias and Sapphira dead. Knowing that the evangelical doctrine of the Bible's infallibility required him to approve of "the atrocities (and treacheries) of Joshua," Lewis made this surprising concession: "The ultimate question is whether the doctrine of the goodness of God or that of the inerrancy of Scripture is to prevail when they conflict. I think the doctrine of the goodness of God is the more certain of the two. Indeed, only that doctrine renders this worship of Him obligatory or even permissible."[3]

In short, Lewis came close to saying that the Supreme Might must live up to moral standards if he is to be regarded as God and not as some cosmic sadist unworthy of worship.

In his letter to the philosopher, Lewis expresses the realization that he could not wholly relativize and trivialize the concept of goodness for the Supreme Being he envisioned:

> To this some will reply "ah, but we are fallen and don't recognize good when we see it." But God Himself does not say that we are as fallen as all that. He constantly, in Scripture, appeals to our conscience: "Why do ye not *of yourselves* judge what is right?"—"What fault hath my people found in me?" And so on. Socrates' answer to Euthyphro is used in Christian form by Hooker. Things are not good because God commands them; God commands certain things because he sees them to be good. (In other words, the Divine Will is the obedient servant to the Divine Reason.) The opposite view (Ockham's, Paley's) leads to an asburdity. If "good" means "what God wills" then to say "God is good" can mean only "God wills what he wills." Which is equally true of you or me or Judas or Satan.[4]

Lewis was not always consistent in his attempt to find a foundation for morality. In some of his earlier books he suggests that God's goodness is incompatible with whatever happens, which, instead of giving theism any advantage over atheism, does little more than make Cosmic Might the personification of moral randomness, of relativism gone out of control.

Recently, I asked a fundamentalist author and apologist who had labeled abortion as murder to tell me whether the killing of pregnant Canaanite women by putative divine decree and Joshua's sword was murder. He replied that the unborn babies killed by Joshua went straight to heaven—which of course does not answer the question of whether God committed *murder* or whether God is above (or below) moral standards. The point here is not to determine whether the fetus is a person but to call attention to the fact that there is considerable moral and ethical relativism in theology and the Bible. Consider this passage from Deuteronomy:

> He whose testicles are crushed or whose male member is cut off shall not enter the assembly of the Lord.
> No bastard shall enter the assembly of the Lord; even to the tenth generation none of his descendants shall enter the assembly of the Lord.
> No Ammorite or Moabite shall enter the assembly of the Lord; even to the tenth generation none belonging to them shall enter the assembly of the Lord for ever. [Deut. 23:1–2 (RSV)]

Whatever the circumstances prompting these prohibitions, it is note-worthy that fundamentalist and evangelical apologists find it necessary to call upon their own version of situation ethics in order to make it clear that not all moral injunctions in the Scriptures are moral absolutes. Evangelical scholar G. T. Manley, in *The New Bible Commentary,* tries to justify the morally inferior outlook found in Deuteronomy by noting that it belongs to "the Mosaic age, and [is] quite different from that of the later monarchy."[5]

Unfortunately, to cast the biblical material in historical context (as doubtless it should be) serves only to emphasize the historical relativism of so-called biblical morality. Indeed, the very notion of a complete and self-consistent biblical morality is problematic. The attempt by some evangelicals to borrow the "progressive revelation" principle in order to make the claim that the later revelation (i.e., the New Testament) stands on a higher plane than the earlier revelation (the Old Testament) collapses when one considers the rage against, and hatred of, most of the human race exemplified in the Book of Revelation. And certainly the threat found in Hebrews 6:4–6—which proclaims that God will never forgive a repentant apostate—is more, not less, vicious than anything found in the Old Testament. When theologians try to justify the vendetta that the Book of Revelation describes in lurid detail, they demonstrate just how perverse the human mind can sometimes become.

Those who believe that the Bible presents its readers moral absolutes have failed to acknowledge the staggering diversity of its moral perspectives. These differing perspectives are often grounded in the political and evangelical experiences of the early Christian church. Professor Daniel Fuller, noted evangelical scholar and former president of Fuller Seminary, pointed out to me, for example, that the apostle Paul had three major problems to face in the early Christian churches: (1) the wall separating Jew and Gentile, (2) the wall separating male and female, and (3) the wall separating slave from free citizen. According to Fuller, Paul, whose theological interpretation of Christ's teachings formed the foundation of the church, felt that he had to make a practical decision to concentrate on the problem of the ethnic and religious relationship between Judaism and Christianity to the exclusion of the other two problems. Fuller's point is that, while racism and sexism are *in principle* undermined by the Christian gospel ("Love thy neighbor as thyself"), Paul was forced to leave to later generations the application of this subversive Christian insight to the problems of racism and sexism. For Paul, getting the church off the ground was the key thing; to try to implement total Christian justice would have scared most potential converts away. I take this to be an example of situation ethics. Whether Paul utilized situation ethics in order to advance the *agape* principle of 1 Corinthians 13 more effectively is a question open for debate. As Morton Smith ably demonstrated in FREE INQUIRY (Spring 1987) there is much in the Bible that contributed to the institution of slavery and little that in actual practice moved against it. Even the Golden Rule of the New Testament, because of its abstractness and adaptability, has throughout history often failed to override the deep-seated racial bigotry of the Book of Genesis.

> The doctrine of election accepted by the Puritans did not incline them to gentleness in their dealing with inferior races. The savage Negroes and the savage Indians were accursed peoples whom it was quite proper to destroy or enslave. "We know not when or how these Indians first became the inhabitants of this mighty continent," says Cotton Mather, "yet we may guess that probably the Devil decoyed these miserable savages hither, in hope that the gospel of the Lord Jesus Christ would never come to destroy or disturb this absolute empire over them."[6]

To be sure, the Bible gives conflicting messages regarding the assimilation of strange peoples. Compare, for example, the books of Ruth and Ezra. The moving and humanistic story of Ruth in the Old Testament is viewed by some scholars as a moral challenge to the Deuteronomic injunction to bar Moabites from the Lord's assembly. The book tells the story of an Israelite man who, because of famine in Israel, chose to move to Moab, taking his wife Naomi with him. The man died, leaving Naomi with two sons, one of whom married Ruth, a Moabite. In time, the two Israelite sons living in Moab died, leaving Naomi with two widowed daughters-in-law. According to this tightly woven story, when the famine in Israel passed and Naomi returned to her homeland, Ruth the Moabitess moved with her, asserting, "Your people shall be my people, and your God my God" (Ruth 1:16 RSV).

The author of the Book of Ruth remarks again and again that Ruth was the Moabitess; she even calls herself "a foreigner." Despite this, Boaz (of Bethlehem in Judah) takes Ruth for his wife. He marries her in part because of the goodness she has shown her mother-in-law, Naomi. Boaz declares that "all my fellow townsmen know that you are a woman of worth" (3:11 RSV).

The story closes with a telling blow against racial bigotry: Ruth has a son, Obed, who in time becomes the grandfather of none other than David himself. So, the Moabitess is the great-grandmother of Israel's most beloved king.

The moral conclusion of the Book of Ezra is less savory. According to Ezra 9 and 10 the Israelite exiles returning from captivity had brought a curse on themselves. God had sent a heavy rain to the land as punishment for their sin of marrying foreign women and bringing them back to pollute the land of Israel. Ezra's solution was simple. Those Israelite men who had foreign (even Moabite) wives should demonstrate their faithfulness to God by putting all these wives away. If the story of Ezra 10 reflects an actual historical period, then we must believe that there was wholesale divorce in the land of Israel during Ezra's time. Indeed, Ezra destroyed more than the marriages. Upon his command, and in the name of God, the men who had married foreign women were forced to separate themselves from their children as well.

It is interesting to see how this kind of moral relativism is perpetuated by evangelical commentaries. In *The New Bible Commentary,* evangelical scholar J. Stafford Wright claims that Ezra's morality should be accorded the status of a norm, the biblical story of Ruth merely an exception to the rule.[7] This strange piece of gerrymandering becomes even more strange when set against the background of the apostle Paul's instruction, which is the opposite of Ezra's. Paul advises the Christian woman who is married to an unbeliever to remain with him as long as he consents to the marriage. Paul then says that the children will greatly benefit by the marriage being kept intact. Ezra's justification for commanding divorce is that the mixed marriage is a pollution or defilement. Paul's justification for advising against divorce is twofold: to provide the Christian with opportunities in marriage to spiritually redeem her or his spouse, and to prevent the children from becoming "unclean" (1 Cor. 7:12–16).

Those who think that the Bible is above situation ethics might find the following worth pondering. In 1 Corinthians 7:20–31, Paul appears to believe that the end of the world is around the corner. In the context of that conviction, the following advice is given: "Every one should remain in the state in which he was called" (1 Cor. 7:20 RSV). Paul elaborates:

> I think that in view of the impending distress it is well for a person to remain as he is. Are you bound to a wife? Do not seek to be free. Are you free from a wife? Do not seek marriage. But if you marry, you do not sin. Yet those who marry will have worldly troubles, and I would spare you that. I mean, brethren, the appointed time has grown very short; from now on, let those who have wives live as thou they had none . . . and those who mourn as though they were not mourning, and those who rejoice as though they were not rejoicing, and those who buy as though they had no goods, and those who deal with the world as though they had no dealings with it. For the form of this world is passing away. [1 Cor. 7:26–31]

It turned out that Paul's judgment of the historical situation was in error. The end was not around the corner, and this miscalculation made his situational advice less than useful. Human miscalculation is one of the weaknesses of situation ethics; but it is a weakness inherent in finite human nature—and it is finite human nature that pervades biblical thought.

My criticism, however, is not of situation ethics. Rather, I criticize those theologians who tell people that biblical ethics advances moral absolutes. In fact, so-called biblical ethics is situation ethics that often sets itself up as immutable divine decree. The unfortunate consequence of this tactic is that moral positions taken in the Bible are denied the useful process of criticism and refinement, a process that is essential if ethics is to escape the brutalizing effects of dogmatism.

NOTES

1. C. S. Lewis, *A Grief Observed* (New York: Seabury Press, 1963), pp. 9–10.

2. July 3, 1963, letter from C. S. Lewis to John Beversluis. Letter quoted in full in John Beversluis, *C. S. Lewis and the Search for Rational Religion* (Grand Rapids: Eerdmans, 1985), pp. 156 f.

3. Ibid., p. 157. Italics added.

4. Cited in ibid., p. 157.

5. G. T. Manley, in *The New Bible Commentary,* 2d ed., F. Davidson, ed. (Grand Rapids: Eerdmans, 1954), p. 215.

6. Thomas J. Wertenbaker, *The First Americans, 1607-1690* (Chicago: Quadrangle Books, 1971), pp. 231 f.

7. J. Stafford Wright, in *The New Bible Commentary,* op. cit., p. 371.

10

Two Kinds of Rights

James Hall

In this essay I will distinguish two significant kinds of rights as they are (or may be) enjoyed by humans. I will give no attention whatever to the occurrence or nonoccurrence of rights outside the human family. That is another issue for another day. The two kinds of rights that I have in mind differ in their ostensible "grounds" or "sources" and, consequently, in their "range" or "extension." I will call them "bestowed rights" and "inherent rights."

PRELIMINARY CLARIFICATIONS

I will begin with some general limts on how I use the term 'rights', independent of the distinction to be explored.

1) As I am using the term, a right is always complemented by some duty. For a person or persons to have a right, is for some person or persons to have a duty. There may be rights that have no such complement, and there certainly may be duties that have no corresponding rights. But I am focusing attention only on whatever kinds of rights *do* have such concomitant outriders. This kind of rights does not occur except in a society of persons. If there were no persons who did or might have a duty toward me, then there would be no one against whom I could assert the kind of rights I want to explore. (One consequence of this: one cannot claim a right to X against those who neither

James Hall is chairman of the Department of Philosophy, University of Richmond.

individually nor collectively have the capacity to do, generate, or distribute *X*. "Ought" still implies "can." A person does not have a right to be fed, for example, when there is no one to feed him or when none of those who *might* feed him *can* feed him.)

2) A right may be either positive or negative. There might, for example, be a right to a minimum annual income, and there might also be a right not to be taxed. I don't believe that either of those putative rights exists. They are only examples of possible rights in the positive and negative modes.

3) A right may be either absolute or *prima facie*. An absolute right is exceptionless while a *prima facie* right is overridable. Some would say that there is a right not to be killed, and claim absolute status for it. Others would say that there is a right to acquire and dispose of material goods as one sees fit, but claim for it only *prima facie,* not absolute, standing. Whether one should accept either of these as a genuine right, whether *prima facie* or absolute, is beside the point. They are transparent enough to illustrate the distinction.

a) Since absolute rights are just that, they know no gradations. Every one of them is just as absolute as every other. But a *prima facie* right has a contingent status in any concrete situation. They may, consequently, be placed in a hierarchical list of descending "importance" or "basicness" and (hence) ascending "overridableness"; and whether one *is* or *is not* legitimately overridable depends, at least in part, on which others are in play in the case.

b) When a right is *prima facie* or overridable, it may not only be overridden by some "higher," "more basic," or "more important" right, but also by considerations of other kinds—usually considerations of overwhelming harm or benefit.

4) A right may or may not be "universal." This is independent of whether or not it is "absolute." Universality is a matter of scope, not overridability.

a) Fairly obviously, a *prima facie* right can have wide, and maybe even universal, scope. (The right of humans not to be killed is arguably universal in its extent in spite of the fact that it is clearly overridable.)

b) Somewhat less obviously, an absolute right can have narrow scope. (A right created by contract might conceivably not be legitimately overridden on any grounds whatever, though, for all its absoluteness, it binds only the parties to the contract.)

c) Certainly a right that is both absolute *and* universal (if one could be found) would be much more impressive than one that is absolute but only narrow-range, *prima facie* but universal, or *prima facie* and narrow-range as well.

5) A right may be either "procedural" or "substantive." A procedural right has to do with the process of actions, not with their content. The opposite is true of substantive rights. (To those of us in the academic life, the process/substance distinction is a commonplace. Whether "due process" is observed in a dismissal procedure is quite distinct from whether there were, in fact, grounds to dismiss.) Preserving procedural rights is often a means of assuring the security of substantive ones. To the extent that this is true, such procedural rights have a certain derivative or instrumental status. On the other hand, it is possible for a procedural right to have nonderivative status. At least one very important (certainly universal and possibly absolute) right is strictly procedural, does not speak directly to the content of actions at all, is "worthwhile" in both derivative and nonderivative fashion, and is crucial to the point of this essay. That right, the right to fair treatment, will be spelled out and discussed presently.

6) Whether or not a particular right exists is at least sometimes independent of whether or not it is known or *recognized.* (*A fortiori,* there is no necessity for a right to be "self-evident." It is always cogent to argue over whether some "x" does or does not really constitute a right. If rights were by their nature "self-evident," such argument would never be cogent.) It is always possible and, with regrettable frequency, it it sometimes actually the case that a *bona fide* right is not yet known, is debated, is ignored, is trampled on, is denied in law and custom, or is otherwise savaged either through ignorance or ill-will. The legitimacy of this point probably will not be fully clear until I have said something about the *origins* of rights. In spite of the fact that it is, now, somewhat cryptic, an example may make the point visible, if not yet convincing: The *prima facie* universal right of human beings not to be bought or sold neither came into existence in the United States with the outlawing of slavery nor is it limited in scope to those societies which have similarly legislated. Note that I am rejecting cultural relativism at this point, at least in so far as certain rights are concerned. I will support this rejection shortly by arguing that at least certain rights, in that they are inherent to a status that is not culturally derived, are not themselves culturally derived.

RIGHTS AS ENTITLEMENTS

The assertion of any right, across the whole spectrum of distinctions that I have mentioned—positive or negative, absolute or *prima facie,* universal or limited, procedural or substantive, recognized or not (unknown, perhaps, or even known but denied, ignored, or otherwise savaged)—makes a distinctive and important kind of moral (i.e., normative behavior) claim: "entitlement." To claim a right is to make a claim of entitlement to some *X* against some person(s). (To *have* a right is to be in a position to make such a claim, whether or not it is, in fact, made.)

1) To claim that *P* is entitled to *X* is to claim far more than that *X* would benefit *P.* There are many things that might benefit an individual to which that individual has no *right.* (I, for one, would be greatly benefited if every citizen in our nation would remit $100 in cash to me today. Not having any leverage on a television network, I have no way to bring that off. But even if I had the leverage, I still would have no *right* to the remittances. Judith Jarvis Thompson's understandable desire for the cool hand of Paul Newman constitutes another example of a benefit to which the beneficiary, as she notes, has no *right,* however beneficial it might be.)

2) To claim that *P* is entitled to *X* is to claim far more than that it would be generally beneficial (over and above any benefit to *P*) if *X* obtained for him or her. While many acts (or restraints from acts) would accrue some general good of some sort, the fact that such general good accrues provides no support by itself for the claim that *P* is *entitled* to the act or restraint. If, for example, all of the disturbed street people in Richmond were fed, clothed, housed, and given complete medical and psychological care, both they and the public at large would derive great good. But it would take far more than that great and general good to establish that the disturbed street people of Richmond had a *right* to such treatment. At the very least, it would require showing that such treatment was *possible.* To restate a point that deserves repetition: "One cannot claim a right to *X* against those who neither individually nor collectively have the capacity to do, generate, or distribute *X.* 'Ought' still implies 'can.'"

3) Sometimes what *P* has a right to is such that getting it would *not* be beneficial (sometimes for *P,* sometimes for others). The possibility of such grave "nonbenefits" provides *one* of the ways in which a right in question may be legitimately overridden ("considerations of massive harm," as noted above). It is, perhaps, my right to retain to my own

use whatever material goods are legitimately within my possession. Retaining those material goods to the significant harm of numbers of persons (say I am the owner of a well-stocked pharmacy, but that I refuse to sell any of my goods to nonwhites—even in a time of severe epidemic), gives us all the example we need of a "right" looking for proper overriding.

4) Successfully to claim entitlement is sometimes (indeed, often) to *prevent* some good. Though a good of some kind is surely achieved when a right is recognized, a possible good of some other kind is often blocked. One typical function of rights is to place a brake on considerations of simple utility. A strong majority may restrain even socially *useful* exploitation of a weak minority by noting the occurrence of certain rights that are incompatible with such exploitation. Thus, judicial framing, slavery in low-technology agrarian economies, and plural marriage might all be blocked by rights considerations in spite of their possible occasional utility.

5) To claim that *P* is entitled to *X* by right is far more than to claim that *P* has license to *X*. License is, in this sense, more closely associated with *privilege* than with *right*. Note, for example, a recent newspaper discussion over whether driving a car on public roads is the exercise of a right or a privilege. The fact that such driving is limited to those who are *licensed* lends at least *prima facie* status to the claim that it is the exercise of a privilege, not a right. One of the most significant differences between rights and privileges is sometimes marked by the presence of an actual license in the latter case—viz., the fact that a privilege can be revoked or withdrawn with the removal of the license of grant. This is not typically true of rights. A full-scale right obtains even when it is not recognized; even when it is ignored or overridden, it is not thereby *revoked*.

THE SOURCES AND BASES OF RIGHTS

To assert that *P* has a right to *X* does not, in and of itself, specify where that right comes from or what the basis of that right might be. Rights can have different sources and/or bases. For that matter, having a source and having a basis are not the same thing. A right can be either acquired or inherent. Acquired rights must come from some source. Inherent rights certainly have a *basis* (typically the nature or the status of those who have them), but do not seem necessarily to have a *source* (except in a stretched sense of the term).

1) An acquired right can come from different sources, e.g., contractual arrangements, general social covenants, laws, customs, sovereign edicts, divine gift, whatever. In any such case we can imagine two persons alike in every way save one, yet where one has the right and the other does not. The simplest requisite difference between them would be that the right has been "bestowed" on one person through the action or intervention of some other event or agent, and has not been "bestowed" on the other. Discovering and specifying a list of such "bestowed" rights in a group can be achieved only by examining the history of decisions, conferrals, habits, and customs there.

2. An inherent right seems to arise intelligibly only from the "character" or the "status" of the people who have them. Being what they are, they have the rights they have—without the necessity of any action or intervention of any agent or event to "bestow" the rights in question on them. Discovering and specifying a list of *these* rights in a group can be achieved only by a painstaking analysis of the varying status that the people there can have.

Sometimes the distinction just observed is blurred. Consider the rights that pertain by law to all the citizens of a nation. At one level of analysis we would call them "inherent" (in that they pertain to anyone and everyone who has the status of citizen in the nation under consideration). They are never bestowed, *as such* on a citizen (even though citizenship itself may be bestowed). At another level of analysis we would call them "acquired" (in that they occur only by virtue of the antecedent decisions in law which establish citizenship and assign rights in terms of it). The blur is readily removable, of course, simply by specifying the level of analysis that concerns us. At the level of "citizen" we clearly have inherent rights—the rights are inherent to the status. At the level of "person" we clearly have acquired ones. Not all persons are citizens; and citizenship itself (and with it all its attendant rights) can be acquired (either by bestowal or by other routes). And the blur will not occur at all if the rights with which we are concerned are rights inherent to a status that is itself not acquired or acquirable.

Whenever we are examining a specific right, we need to exercise some care to note whether it is inherent or acquired *at the level of analysis that concerns us*. This is important for a number of reasons, not the least of which is that the possibility, or at any rate the ease, of revocability of a right is a function of its status as inherent or acquired, especially if the acquisition is by bestowal.

A bestowed acquired right is more similar to a licensed privilege than is an inherent right, in that it is easily revocable and an inherent right is not. It can be revoked by cancelling, rescinding, or withdrawing the action that bestows it. (For example, if the civil law grants certain rights to those who own property, it may just as easily retract them, or even decline to grant them in the first place.) But the only way in which an inherent right could be revoked would be by cancelling the status to which it is inherent. (For example, if certain rights were inherent to property owners, then they could only be retracted by doing away with the status of property ownership altogether.)

THE INHERENT RIGHTS OF PERSONS

One cannot have a status without having along with it whatever rights are inherent to that status. One does not have to wait to acquire a right, *a fortiori* for it to be *bestowed,* if the right in question is inherent to a status that one already possesses. Of course, if one is unfortunate enough to live in a society that does not recognize, or ignores, the rights that one has, then one may have to wait for cultural changes to occur in order to *exercise* the rights in question. But one still *has* those rights. While there is nothing necessarily morally wrong about refusing to bestow a right, there are all sorts of things necessarily morally wrong about failing to recognize, observe, or respect an inherent right.

Whatever rights may be inherent to the status of persons pertain to all who are persons, and can be ignored only at the moral peril of those who ignore them. Persons do not acquire these rights or strive to acquire them. Individuals do not wait for them to be bestowed by law, custom, or edict. They simply *have* them. They may have to strive very hard, of course, to get them recognized!

I have already noted that *certain* statuses are, themselves, acquirable. Thus, if an acquirable status has certain rights that are inherent to it, then those rights can, of course, be (in a sense) acquired. Thus, if we are examining the inherent rights of *citizens* in a given society, we must note that since "citizenship" is itself a conventional and acquirable status, the rights inherent to it are only universal to *that* set of individuals (i.e., they may be acquired by those who achieve the status, and they may be lost if the status itself can be lost).

On the other hand, when we consider the inherent rights of *persons,* unless "personhood" is a conventional and acquirable status, we need not worry about how to achieve (or avoid losing) those rights inherent thereto. But "personhood" is neither conventional nor acquired. It is a matter of function and capacity, and it obtains wherever those functions and capacities obtain. Recognition of that status may well follow certain culturally determined conventions; but we have already seen that whether or not a right is recognized is an entirely distinct question from whether or not it obtains. And the same is true of those statuses to which rights attach.

It is possible, of course, for persons to have no inherent rights. I would claim that there is at least one such right (fairness); but I do recognize that this claim is arguable. Nevertheless, *if* there are any rights whatever inherent to the status of persons, then they are *universal* to that set by the very meaning of *inherent*.

FAIRNESS

I have twice suggested that something like a right to fairness is inherent to persons. To treat individual *P fairly* is to treat *P* in exactly the same way that you treat every individual who is relevantly indistinguishable from *P*. To say that people have a right to fairness, then, is to say that they are entitled to such nondiscriminatory treatment.

In the negative mode: if you treat two people differently, then you are treating them unfairly unless there is a real difference between them that is relevant to the discrimination and unless the degree of discrimination is commensurate to the degree of objective difference. If a father buys a pair of mittens for each of his blue-eyed children, but lets his brown-eyed ones go out in the cold bare-handed, then *ceteris paribus* he is treating them unfairly. If, on the other hand, he provides a pair for each of his two-handed children, only one mitten for each of his one-handed children, and none at all to the unfortunate one who lost both arms at the elbows in a trolley-car accident, then *ceteris paribus* he is not (at least in the matter of mittens) being unfair to them at all. (I am ignoring matters of size and handedness only for the sake of brevity.)

When one does discriminate, claiming that there is an objective basis of difference for the discrimination, the burden of proof is on he who discriminates to give cogent evidence of that claimed objective basis. Further, when an objective basis of difference is demonstrated, a second burden of proof exists to give cogent evidence that it is *relevant* to the difference in treatment. Further, when an objective and relevant basis of difference is demonstrated, the burden of proof demands that cogent evidence be provided showing the *degree* of difference in treatment to be commensurate with the justifying basis in fact.

That is what the right to fairness amounts to. It is clearly a procedural right. It has both positive and negative aspects. It is *prima facie* (over-ridable), not absolute. And, since it is *inherent* to the status of person, it is universal to the class of persons. It is not acquired. It need not be bestowed. It is regularly ignored, denied, and savaged. And those who ignore, deny, and savage it are morally condemnable thereby.

I make no claim that this alleged universal human right is self-evident. I do argue, however, that it *is* evident upon consideration: 1) To operate without it is incoherent in the sense that it is arbitrary and capricious. 2) To operate without it is also to cut the ground from under any talk of *substantive* rights (whether inherent or acquired). How can Paul have a right not to be killed if Peter (who is relevantly indistinguishable from him) does not? How can Mary have a right to sell her house if Martha (who, with her house, is "just like" Mary and hers) does not?

If people have any rights at all, they have *this* right. Of course, maybe they don't have any rights at all. But the consensus of contemporary secular morality is that people *do* have some rights. And, that being the case, it follows that modern secular morality is committed to the notion of an inherent human right to fair treatment.

THE POINT OF THE ESSAY

What does all of this have to do with putative contrasts between secular and biblical morality? Simply this: the notion of an inherent human right to fairness, which is a commonplace in contemporary secular morality, is not to be found in the biblical ethic at all. This particular inherent human right is not to be found there because no notion of any inherent human right whatever is to be found there. I do not argue that no notion whatever of right is in the Bible, though in fact this may be the case. Rather I only argue that whatever attention to rights may be found there is necessarily limited to *acquired* and, more specifically, *bestowed* rights.

Of course I do not argue that no notions of *morality* are to be found in the Bible. They are. Lots of them: notions of morality and law, morality and grace, morality and covenants, morality and justice, morality and mercy, morality and love; but nowhere morality and the inherent rights of humans.

1) From a biblical perspective, even the status of being human is a bestowed status. Presuming that there is a creator, then obviously every *status* is a bestowed *status* in as absolute a sense of "bestowed" as there can be. Whatever *rights* are inherent to the human status (whether any are mentioned are not) are themselves acquired only with the status acquisition. But in the contemporary secular conception of mankind, our human status is the starting point. Neither it nor any of its attached rights are acquired, much less bestowed.

2) In the biblical perspective, the basic cosmological model is essentially monarchical. In monarchical systems, absolute ones at any rate, *all* statuses except that of the monarch himself are bestowed, and any rights that do occur are clearly by sufferance of the monarch. From everything we know about earthly monarchies, any and all grantable rights are equally revocable. It would certainly seem to follow that if God stands to men as a king stands to his subjects (unless, Heaven forfend, God is a constitutional monarch) then any rights that obtain for men do so only contingently and at the will of the bestower.

3) In the biblical accounts, God does enter into covenants with "His people." Perhaps those covenants can be read as creating or bestowing rights of certain kinds. (Indeed, I think they can; and this is why I do not argue that there is no biblical notion of rights at all.) But the covenants are not universal, hence the rights generated in them are not universal. Thus, rights are not inherent to persons, but only contingently enjoyed by the particular persons who happen to be covered or "chosen."

4) Anything that is bestowed can be revoked; and any covenant entered into can be abrogated (or at the very least replaced by a new one). Any property of P that is unilaterally revocable, abrogable, or replaceable by another fails utterly to be an inherent right of P.

5) Many specific human rights commonly recognized by contemporary secular moralists appear to be missing in the biblical account. Not even the *prima facie* right not to be killed is uniformly secure. At the very best it might pertain to members of the covenant group (and certainly not to Canaanites et al.). In fact, even with the establishment of the first covenant, and long before the promulgation of the law, the *prima facie* right not to be killed did not appear secure even for the children of the most favored. When Abraham turns his knife aside, it is *not* because his son has a substantial right against

such homicidal conduct, but rather because human sacrifices "are not pleasing" to the God of the mountains. To be sure, there is a later commandment to do no murder; but even there the *grounds* are in the *command* and not in the rights of potential victims.

6) Where kindness to the alien *is* biblically encouraged it is either seen as mercy or as a work of *agape,* not as a duty generated by the indigenous rights of the aliens themselves. In the more ancient writings, of course, little kindness to the alien is encouraged; and certainly no *rights* are recognized. By modern secular standards, even the hapless inhabitants of the "promised land" had *some* rights (both inherent ones as humans and derived ones as law-abiding property holders). But they fell before swords wielded by men with a different concept of the good.

7) The biblical God Himself is noted for justice and mercy, not for rights recognition. He kept bargains, perhaps; but there are only contract-derived rights at work here. The inherent right of a person to fair treatment is not a contract-based *quid pro quo.*

8) Even the famous passage about there being "neither Jew nor Greek" in the eventual kingdom is not a recognition of inherent human rights, *a fortiori* the inherent human right to fair treatment. All that we have here is the substitution of one set of possibly arbitrary bestowal criteria for another set of obviously arbitrary bestowal criteria. Before the new Heaven and new Earth, rights (if there are any at all) are clearly ethnic-group and gender based. That is transparently unfair. In the new Heaven and new Earth they will be creed based. No increase in fairness is obvious here.

9) If one accepts the notion that (perhaps due to original sin) all persons are totally (and equally) depraved and consequently equitably, naturally, and uniformly destined to torment and destruction (having *no* redeeming features whatever), then clearly nobody has much of a substantive right to *any* benefits. The justice will be horrendous but fair; and only undeserved mercy dispensed by grace will save anyone at all. This, of course, denies the occurrence of any substantive rights (other than the "right" to universally earned punishment). If the factual suppositions were accurate, then that might be fair enough; but the ensuing grace that blesses the chosen few flies in the face of even a minimal notion of procedural fairness.

10) It is hard sometimes, of course, to remember what is biblical and what is not. When one notes some of the religious apparatus in which revolutionary American ideals were fleshed out, one cannot ignore the stirring reference to the way in which all men are noted to have

been endowed by their Creator with certain rights. And there is a consequent tendency to read that back into the documentary basis of the common religious tradition. Wasn't it the God of the Bible that endowed us with those rights? So aren't those rights derived from the religion of the Bible? So aren't those rights biblical? Ignore all the bad reasoning; but don't ignore the fact that even there it is a matter of *endowment* or *bestowal,* and not a matter of recognizing any inherent rights at all.

CONCLUSION

Biblical ethics and modern secular ethics differ radically. The latter recognizes—indeed, is predicated on—the recognition of inherent human rights, and the former (where it implies rights at all) encompasses only externally bestowed ones. Even if biblical concepts included (as bestowed) every substantive right that modern ethics teaches (as inherent), the possibility of revocation, which is unelminable from acquired rights, marks the two views as radically different.

Most crucially, unless those who assign human fates in terms of "what you believe" can bear the burden of proof that this is a real and relevant criterion for differentiating persons, the biblical account (even at its highest) has not a shred of what contemporary secular moralists surely insist is one of the few items at the core of all morality: the inherent procedural human right to fairness.

All that I have really shown is that the modern secular view of ethics and the biblical view are *different* on the question of inherent rights. It is entirely possible that the modern secular view of ethics is wrong and that the biblical view is right. It has not been my task to prove beyond question the objective reality of any inherent rights, *a fortiori* the objective reality of a universal *prima facie* human right to fairness.

LAST REMARKS

1) The presence or absence of a notion of the right to fairness marks every dimension of an ethical scheme. Whatever virtues the biblical scheme may have (including the virtue of truth, if it has it), that scheme does not have a notion of an inherent human right to fairness, and

its absence shows vividly. Given that it is difficult to get people to recognize the rights of others, and given the tremendous influence that the Bible is said to have on people, one could wish that this notion were not excluded. If it were there, it might speak to the religious and political blood feuds that so plague our present world and that draw much of their fuel from the notion that those who are "beyond the pale" have no rights at all. But, of course, if it were there it would be blithely ignored as are all the parts that the inerrantists already ignore.

2) There is one reasonable, modern religious riposte to all of this that must be mentioned before I conclude. Surely it is the case that even a traditionally understood God (omnipotence being understood in terms of the ability to do anything that can be done) could not create a person without thereby creating an *X* that has the inherent right to fair treatment. That is, I think, a reasonable theological insight into the nature of God (one worthy of worship) and of the consistent possibilities of creation. If that is the case, then clearly a reasonable theological or religious morality does not necessarily exclude the essential concept of inherent rights, which modern secular ethics has and biblical ethics lacks. So it follows that one *can* (at least on this score) maintain a *religious,* even if not a *biblical,* ethic incorporating fairness (and maybe even some other notions of inherent human rights). The point, of course, is that an enlightened and morally sensitive concept of religion therefore *cannot* confine itself to a conception of the Bible as its *limit.* And that is as good a place to stop as any.

11

The Morality of God and the Morals of Inerrancy

Some Thoughts on Justice, Compassion, Peace, and Freedom

Robert S. Alley

As a child I recall owning a Bible story book. It was a blue book with large pages and many vivid illustrations. One story in particular caught my fancy; one picture remains etched in my mind. In simple language the tale of Noah was recounted, and opposite one printed page was a depiction of the flood with Noah standing imperiously on the bow of the Ark observing a distressed mother clutching the slender branch of a tree top just barely above water level. She was holding a tiny baby aloft in a last effort to save the child. I thought then, as I think now, that whatever "sins" that woman had committed, she was possessed of infinitely more compassion, love, and humanity than the pious Noah surveying the rising tide with "I told you so" on his mind. And by clear logic that woman was far more worthy of adoration than the god to whom Noah gave allegiance.

I am aware that this biblical account may be integrated into a grand theological design in which the Genesis myth is understood as a reflection upon an ancient cosmic inquiry. Yet, for the communicant in the pew it remains as morally suspect as the punishment meted out to Daniel's enemies. When the tale is gilded with an inerrantist brush the result is moral perversion. Since such stories are the stock in trade

---

Robert S. Alley is professor of humanities at the University of Richmond.

of hundreds of volunteer Sunday school teachers who have read neither Walther Eichrodt nor Gerhard von Rad, the malicious mischief imposed upon generations of children is evident.

When in a public school in Henrico County, Virginia, my son was exposed in first grade to extensive commentary about the Bible. I became aware of this unconstitutional outrage when, at dinner one evening, I was asked whether God ever killed people. When I responded negatively there was clear upset in my son's eyes. His teacher had informed him that god killed an entire population in the flood. It had clearly disturbed him, a fact that identified his ethics as considerably more advanced than those of his teacher or the god she grandly waved before five year olds.

I employ these anecdotes to make a quite simple point: The biblical material from Genesis to Revelation, apart from constructive critical analysis, easily becomes the text for an ethic of vengeance, violence, discrimination, and injustice. The biblical inerrantist, voluntarily trapped in a morass of moral blindness that condones slavery, genocide, racism, holy war, sexism, and revenge, compounds the problem by seeking support for his or her interpretations from church "fathers" like Thomas Aquinas, Augustine, Martin Luther, and John Calvin. These are men who have already read into their theologizing a culturally conditioned moral myopia. The wise and profound insights about the divine nature to be discovered in the words of Isaiah, Amos, and Hosea are vitiated by a theory that requires the believer to accept all biblical affirmations about God as being of equal quality. Such a view reduces their god to a reflection of ancient cultural norms. In the process, the biblical writings are translated from an evolving record of religious encounters to an obscene distortion. It belittles those early searchers for meaning, forever incarcerating their inquiries in a prison of contradictions.

Such is the result of asserting, as Adrian Rogers, president of the Southern Baptist Convention, recently did, that the Bible is completely free of error or contradiction. Now Mr. Rogers can believe any silly thing he wishes, but the implications of his public remarks bear scrutiny. Not long ago, the presidents of the six Southern Baptist seminaries have surrendered to this irrational view of the Bible. In so doing they have abandoned reason, faculties, honor, and scholarship.

It is easy enough to understand this problem when dealing with the prehistoric myths and legends of Genesis or the primitive ethic of unbridled nationalism. It is less obvious, perhaps, in the case of Christian theology having to do with the mythologized life of Jesus. Take, for example, the long-standing affirmation of Mary's virginal conception of Jesus. As Don Cuppitt has noted: "However the belief arose it has done great harm. It has suggested that Jesus was not an ordinary man, it has helped to poison people's feelings about the process of reproduction, and it has encouraged ugly and useless forms of asceticism."[1] It must be added, belief in the virgin birth has generated a church-sponsored sexism evident today in both fundamentalism and papal decree.

For a few minutes let us consider the morality of a god encased in the straitjacket of biblical inerrancy. I will not consume your time by pointing to the myriad of ways in which such a view tangles the believer in a web of practical contradictions. Rather, let us explore what type of god these inerrantists offer.

Consider the morality of a god who responds to a prayer by Pat Robertson and in so doing redirects the path of a hurricane. At least two points are clear. If Robertson's god did respond to the prayer, then that deity's initial intent was the destruction of life and property in Virginia Beach. Only Robertson's superior morality was able to change the heart of a vengeful god. (The same logic applies to the healing antics of the religious right to which I shall return shortly.) But we have a second problem. Robertson appears not to have requested, and his god seemed uninterested in, sparing the people of New England. Robertson's god then appears to operate upon a Pentagon inspired tactic. Virginia Beach was god's primary target. A heavy cloud cover of witnesses made that impractical so god dumped his load on the less strategic, secondary target, of New England.

It is interesting to speculate about what this type of god might have accomplished were he in possession of the insights of a cadre of Pat Robertsons. The smiling parson from Virginia sees the nation as plagued by secular humanism and other similar rancid evils. Why has god avoided a preemptive strike?

The moral corruption of biblical inerrantists is exhibited most clearly when Christianity, identifying itself as the exclusive witness to truth, seeks to join forces with the state. Defining the new order with the inerrantist motif, men like Falwell, Criswell, Swaggert and Robertson commandeer a diverse cultural heritage in the name of their image of Jesus. In alliance with the power of government, these men direct hatred toward all those who espouse different visions. The ethic of the caring carpenter is translated into nationalistic bombast and, as Cuppitt observes, "The religion of a condemned criminal, rejected of men, now itself condemns criminals in his name."

If those with a different vision reject the Bible as final authority, they are singled out for elimination from the body politic. Since the public schools offer a microcosm of our pluralistic, secular society, these institutions become a primary target for annihilation. Here inerrantist morality coincides with jingoistic nationalism: the so-called good of the state and the approved faith condone any form of dishonesty and deceit. Now, as devoted as many are to secular humanism, they know that the vast majority of public school teachers are not part of that movement. Fundamentalists know this as well. Whatever the character of our neighborhoods and communities, that character is reflected in the underpaid teaching staff of the local public school. Those teachers are our friends, neighbors, and relatives. What they have in common with humanists, secular and otherwise, is a commitment to the principle of a nonreligious, neutral environment for learning in our pluralistic democracy. Fundamentalists will have none of this, and will abandon any canon of truth to destroy the idea. The recent decision in the Tennessee textbook case identifies the ultimate goal—destruction of the public school system.

No representation of a deity in our time has been more clearly the reflection of human pride and arrogance than that proudly unfurled by Pat Robertson. If there were such a divine being as Robertson describes, it would be one so inferior to humanistic ethics as to be unworthy of anything other than derision. Robertson worships a god who is a remarkable reflection of himself.

Unfortunately, religious leadership in our day has been all too often identified with persons reflecting inerrantist, legalistic perspectives. This is compounded by the self-styled moderate church leaders who continue to adhere to church dogma with a practical inerrantism that "protects" the faithful from modern insights. Thus is the mainstream of Christianity made impotent.

Inerrantists are not content with literalism as a practical application. It is too subjective. One person's literal interpretation might vary from that of a neighbor. There must be a norm or standard for the faithful. No priesthood of believers here! To give an example, let us consider Robertson's assertion that the book of Ezekiel mentions the United States. Not all inerrantists would concur, so who is to decide what their god meant when he dictated "the young men of Tarshish"? The answer appears to be spiritual arrogance. If Robertson says it loud enough perhaps he can even convince God.

All of us read into our most prized trove of thought our own biases. I hear what I most want to hear: in Amos' words, "Let justice roll down like waters, and righteousness like an ever-flowing stream" (5:24). Hubert Humphrey used that verse as a justification for his views on racial equality. In the interaction between ancient thinkers and rational, humanistic modern readers there comes a moment of creative cooperation of ideas. We then seek to implement our beliefs, invigorated, as they may have been, by earlier ideas. The difference with the inerrantist comes at this point.

If one is committed to freedom of conscience then Thomas Jefferson becomes an ancient voice of insight to whom one responds. However, the humanist is reminded by historical research that the sage of Monticello had serious shortcomings in his treatment of slavery. A natural selection of ideas occurs. We can examine the moral insights of our human kin from the past, while recognizing their frailty. This in turn makes us instantly aware of our own proclivities toward self-serving moral blindness.

The biblical inerrantist has found a way to short circuit this process of moral growth by establishing, on the authority of human witnesses alone, an absolute norm for all humanity. Any agreement with what is described as ethical relativism corrupts the system, so the fundamentalist inerrantist must recite biblical authority as the foundation for his version of situation ethics. The trap is sprung and the cultural and societal practices of long lost civilizations become sources of current fundamentalist ethical norms. The nature of their god was preformed in a world we cannot know and only vaguely comprehend. Any dynamic view of the deity is, we are assured by fundamentalists, abandoned to the prison of biblical inerrantism. But the proponents are not serious. They have a modern moral agenda, one that requires a guru, a priest, or a television evangelist to explain with "holy writ." Such a one, of course, chooses the texts and constructs a moral system according to his or her own designs, the Bible serving as a convenient charm.

In pre-Civil War times, "frantically concerned to repel the charge that slaveholding was necessarily a sin, the southern preacher seized upon every crumb of scripture that might possibly support his argument."[2] In so doing, the apologists for slavery insisted that to denounce the practice was "to impugn God's word." Biblical inerrantism took wing with Methodist Alexander McCaine who said of Noah's remarks in Genesis 9:25: "He spoke under the impulse and dictation of Heaven. His words ('cursed be Canaan; a slave of slaves shall he be to his brothers') were the words of God himself, and by them was slavery ordained. This was an early arrangement of the Almighty, to be perpetuated through all time."[3] Jesus was likewise enlisted by a literal reading of parables, such as the master-slave story in Luke 17:7–10. The final bastion of biblical endorsement for slavery came from Paul. It needs to be made clear that the answer to such nonsense does not lie in claiming that the Bible endorses emancipation. It clearly does not, and there is ample evidence that biblical writers accepted the fact of slavery without protest. A reverse inerrantism is no good. A forthright assertion that the authors of Genesis and Paul were wrong is the only means to retain the Bible as a viable document.

Inerrantists are fond of using the Adam and Eve story to endorse sexism. Opponents misstep when, in good faith and seeking to rescue God from such theory, they insist that the Bible supports sexual equality. Such a response suggests that the "liberal" in this debate has equal need of some inerrant authority or dogma. Would we not expect male writers of 800 B.C.E. to 100 C.E. to reflect a sexist bias? Feminist theologians search in the wrong places when they seek androgyny in Genesis and Paul. And if God dictated to those authors, then the deity is sexist to the core.

By the moral standards of the churches of Martin Luther and the Spanish Inquisition, the only fault to be found with Adolf Hitler was his inadequate follow-through. From whence did that morality emerge? It came from the exclusive claim to truth about the gentle Jesus, a claim that demanded acceptance of him as divine on penalty of death— always spiritual but all too often physical. As one reads Luther's anti-Semitic ravings, the biblical justifications abound. His 1543 treatise "On the Jews and Their Lies" is laced with biblical quotations.

Inerrantists of all stripes appear to have developed a strategy for social control to which they apply the canons of their scriptures. Religious documents in their first generation have the freshness of spiritual encounter. Institutions to which these documents were not addressed then apply them to situations totally foreign to their origins. Later, clergy read back into the "holy writ" intentions of their god respecting the development of the institution that established the writings as sacred to begin with.

Finally, there is faith healing. This spiritual alchemy offends the sensitivities of caring humanists of all traditions. Trading on fear and ignorance, self-styled healers like Pat Robertson draw upon biblical phrases born in another culture to claim the power of the deity to heal the sick. Biblical inerrantism makes this one easy, for there are so many references to this phenomenon in the New Testament. The stories about Jesus on this subject are probably a combination of credulity, world view, and wishful reconstruction. Nowhere is the biblical critic more desperately needed than in this arena. Watch for a few moments the way in which Pat Robertson and others employ the Bible to effect a control over an audience that they then willfully manipulate.

Biblical inerrantism vitiates the ethical progress of religious people of all faiths, along with that of persons whose ethical standards emerge from alternative sources. Non-Christian and Christian humanists alike are accused of being blinded to human traits that betray the principles of justice, freedom, compassion, and love. These denunciations of alternatives to inerrantism stem from a need to strengthen the institution. "To make the Church strong you must prove that it matters a great deal whether people belong to the Church or not and you must show that through the labors of the Church, people can be rescued from damnation."[4] In contrast, most humanists concur with the thought expressed by Franklin Roosevelt: "The fight for social justice and economic Democracy . . . is a long, weary, uphill struggle." The importance lies with the concept of human struggle, one that unites those citizens of all persuasions who share a common commitment to the democratic principles inherent in our secular Republic. This is a far cry from those pathetically frightened Tennessee parents who see so great a danger in the human capacities for courage, cognition, and compassion that they would ban *The Wizard of Oz*.

The consequence of all this is a critical need for serious biblical scholarship. And this is not confined to those affiliated with synagogues and churches. The woeful ignorance of the public concerning the Bible, coupled with the book's near magical character in much of our cultural heritage, creates a serious challenge to every competent historian and literary critic. The task is one of demystification that will allow the book to remain central to the lives of the faithful while identifying its true character as a record of religious experiences. Such a scientific endeavor, divested of cant, would, I think, be a genuine exercise of contemporary morality.

NOTES

1. Don Cuppitt, *Crisis of Moral Authority: The Dethronement of Christianity* (Lutterworth Press, 1972), p. 154.

2. H. Shelton Smith, *In His Image, But* . . .(Durham, N.C.: Duke University Press, 1972), p. 130.

3. Alexander McCaine, *Slavery Defended From Scripture,* 1842.

4. Cuppitt, p. 103.

12

Japan and Biblical Religion
The Religious Significance of the
Japanese Economic Challenge

Richard L. Rubenstein

Few, if any, developments in the post-war era possess as great a potential for world-historical significance as the rise of Japan. Normally, Japan's rise is discussed in economic or political terms. Its religious significance, especially for a nation such as the United States, whose cultural inheritance is so deeply rooted in biblical religion, is seldom discussed, much less understood. Japan is the world's most successful nation with non-Christian roots. Even the Soviet Union has Christian roots. Marxist atheism is grounded in the very biblical tradition that Marxism negates. Moreover, the apparent conflict between the Western proponents of a biblically-grounded and a secular ethic takes on the appearance of a family quarrel when seen against the horizon of Japanese religion and culture. Far from being the antithesis of biblical religion, the secular spirit that pervades so much of Western life is its unintended consequence. Wherever the biblical faith in a unique, exclusive extramundane God penetrated, it was utterly destructive of indigenous gods and traditions. Sooner or later this polemic, desacralizing faith was bound to give birth to a consciousness that would not rest until *all* the gods without exception were dethroned. Under the circumstances, it is hardly surprising that a civilization as determined to preserve its own integrity as that of Japan would marshall all of its forces to resist both the believing and the secular manifestations of biblical religion.

Richard L. Rubenstein is professor of religion at Florida State University.

The Japanese have created a thoroughly modern, high-technology civilization whose religious foundations rest upon animistic and polythestic traditions that adherents of the biblical religions normally assume to be discredited, primitive, and idolatrous—a remnant of a far earlier stage of religious "evolution." From the Japanese perspective, such views are, of course, utterly without substance.

We can perhaps best understand the long-range significance of the Japanese religious challenge—and it is a challenge—if we consider the role of religion in fostering the modernization of both Japan and the nations of the West. In the case of the West, no attempt to understand the role of religion in the formation of the modern world can ignore the work of the German sociologist Max Weber. As is well known, Weber set forth the thesis that the modern Western bourgeois-capitalist world is an unintended consequence of the rise of ascetic Protestantism in the aftermath of the Reformation.[2]

Weber did not hold that religion by itself was the cause of modern capitalism. He regarded religion as a necessary but not a sufficient factor in the origin of modern economic rationalism. Weber stressed that material conditions alone could not have produced the peculiar form of economic rationalism in which the impulse to accumulate was combined with disciplined restraints upon consumption. Nor could capitalism by itself have produced the kind of economic ethic needed for its development. As is well known, Weber held that the economic ethic that fostered the development of capitalism was an unintended consequence of the work of the great reformers, especially John Calvin, and their followers.

According to Weber, Calvin's doctrine of double predestination was of crucial importance for the development of modern capitalism. By insisting that the issue of personal salvation had been settled at the very first moment of creation, Calvinism had the effect of radically devaluing the religious significance of all earthly institutions including the church. The believer was thrust back upon himself with no assurance of where he stood before an awesome, inscrutable, and utterly sovereign God. The believer's situation was further aggravated by the fact that there was no longer any credible mediating agency authorized to prescribe the conditions under which an individual, aided by god's grace, might merit salvation. Concerning the impact of predestination, Weber observes:

> In its extreme inhumanity this doctrine must above all have had one
> consequence to the generation that surrendered to its magnificent

consistency. That was a feeling of unprecedented inner loneliness of the single individual.[3]

Under the circumstances, it was inevitable that the believer seek for some hint of where he or she stood in the divine order. According to Weber, at this point economic activity took on a new meaning for the believing Protestant.

Service in one's worldly calling, even if it involved deriving profit from money itself, soon came to be regarded as offering the believer a sign of where he or she stood before the Creator.[4] A believer who had prospered in his calling could reasonably assume that the God who had predestined all things from the beginning had been the ultimate cause of his or her well-being. The sober, methodical accumulation of wealth took on a religious meaning it had never before possessed. Thus, methodical work within the profane world became the path to overcoming anxiety concerning one's ultimate destiny, which prayer, ritual, and mystical contemplation had been in other traditions.

The radical devaluation of the normal religious media of redemption by ascetic Protestantism was part of a process identified by Weber as the "disenchantment of the world," by which he meant that "there are no mysterious incalculable forces that come into play, but rather one can, in principle, master all things by calculation."[5] According to Weber, the roots of this disenchantment, which was indispensable to the development of the distinctive rationalism of the modern world, were to be found in the monotheistic exclusivity of biblical Judaism.[6] By affirming a unique, supramundane creator God, biblical Judaism denied any inherent sacrality to the natural world or to the political order. God alone was regarded sacred. There were no longer any divine spirits inherent in nature to be appeased, supplicated, or magically manipulated. Nor was there anything inherently sacred about the political order. Of special interest with regard to Japan is the fact that *biblical religion was especially vehement in its rejection of the institution of divine kingship*. The biblical injunction, "Thou shalt have no other gods before me" (Exod. 20:3), was as much a political statement rejecting the divine kings of Egypt and the ancient Near East as it was a denial of animism, magic, and polytheism.[7] Rejecting magic, animism, and polytheism, the Bible's radical desacralization of both the natural and the political order was thus an enormously significant step toward the rational mastery of the world.

Nevertheless, before the rationalizing activities of the modern era, such as the creation of an impersonal market economy, scientific investigation, and bureaucratic organization, could become culturally predominant, these activities had to be given a religiously legitimated, positive valence. Weber argued that this only became possible after ascetic Protestantism had redefined worldly activity, including the taking of interest, as a way of serving God. Neither rationalization nor Protestantism's interpretation of worldly activity as a sacred calling could by itself have brought about modern capitalism. Only the combination of the two could have provided the "take-off" energies that made capitalism possible in the West.

The development toward a purely secular, rationalized society can thus be seen as an unintended sociological consequence of biblical Judaism's "disenchantment of the world." However, Judaism's marginal position in the Christian West limited its ability to influence the latter's development. The full force of biblical "disenchantment" was only felt after Protestantism elevated the authority of the Bible over that of the church.

From a social-psychological perspective, Protestantism's rejection of the authority of the church can be seen as a revolt of the sons against the fathers. A similar revolt was indispensable for the successful displacement of traditional society by modern civilization. According to sociologist Robert Bellah, biblical religion provided the legitimation that made these revolts ethically and psychologically acceptable. Bellah's argument takes as its starting point a comparison of the father-son symbolism in Christianity and Confucianism.[8] According to Bellah, although the father-son symbolism plays a decisive role in Christianity, the natural family has little or no religious significance. By contrast, the father-son symbolism is inapplicable to the Ultimate in Confucianism whereas the natural family has overwhelming religious significance.

Contrary to both popular and Freudian belief, the biblical God was not originally a father-God but the ultimate suzerain of a political association. The Bible does not depict God's relation to Israel as the head of a natural family or as an originating ancestor. His relation took the form of a political treaty between a suzerain and his vassal. In the ancient Near East this type of treaty was known as a *b'rith* or covenant. In such a pact the superior party stipulates the conditions under which he will protect the inferior party as well as the penalties to be incurred for a lack of fidelity to the terms of the treaty. Indeed, contemporary scholars have come to see the biblical covenant as modeled after Hittite treaties of the fourteenth and thirteenth centuries, B.C.E.[9]

Isaiah ben-Dasan, a perceptive Japanese writer who took an Israeli pseudonym, has also argued that the divine-human relation in biblical religion could not be understood on the analogy of the relation between a natural parent and child. Ben-Dasan did not stress the political character of the relationship. Instead, he argued that the relation was that "between adopted child and adoptive parent," God being the adoptive parent and Israel the adopted child.[10] By thus depicting the divine-human relationship, biblical religion introduced an element of insecurity and anxiety into Western religious life. Unlike the unconditional relationship between a natural parent and child, that between an adoptive parent and adopted child is likely to be conditioned upon the fulfillment of contractual obligations involved in the adoption process. As Ben-Dasan reminds us, adoption is a parent-child relation established by contract. This is in fact how the Bible depicts God's relationship with Israel. The conditional character of the relationship is repeatedly stated. For example, Moses solemnly warns the Children of Israel lest they fail to observe God's commandments:

> But if you do not obey the Lord your God by diligently observing all his commandments and statutes which I lay upon you this day, then all these maledictions shall come to you and light upon you. (Deut.28:15)

This admonition is followed by the terrible list of chastisements that await those who disobey Israel's God.

Both Judaism and Roman Catholicism, each in its own way, sought to mitigate the potential harshness of the divine-human relationship. By insisting upon the unadorned, literal reading of scripture, ascetic Protestantism rejected all such mitigations. By contrast, there is no sovereign, personal Creator God in Confucianism. Instead, the Tao refers to the cosmic harmony of Heaven, Earth, and man; there is nothing comparable to Christianity's use of the father-son metaphor. Nevertheless, insofar as religious life is founded upon the family and the ancestor cult in Confucianism, there is a coincidence between the sphere of the family and that of religion, which is absent from biblical religion. Similarly, Ben-Dasan points out that the Japanese find distasteful the biblical idea of God as an adoptive parent. They regard their relationship with their deities as one of blood, like that of mother and child, as in the tradition of the descent of the emperor from the Sun Goddess, Amaterasu-omi-kami.

In the Biblical traditions, religion and the family are represented by a common set of symbols yet they are institutionally differentiated.

While filial piety is a supreme virtue in Confucianism, both Christianity and Judaism tend to devalue filial piety when it conflicts with the imperatives of religion. The case of Christianity is the more obvious. Baptism, the rite by which one is initiated into the Christian church, is in principle destructive of filial piety. In baptism one dies to one's old natural self and to one's old familial relations, and is reborn a new being in Christ. Thus, Paul writes,

> Are you ignorant of that when we were baptized in Christ Jesus we were baptized in his death? In other words, when we were baptized we went into the tomb with him and joined him in death, so that as Christ was raised from the dead by the Father's glory, we too might live a new life. (Rom. 6:3, 4)[11]

Similarly, Jesus is depicted as admonishing his followers to "hate father and mother, wife and children, brothers and sisters" as an indispensable condition of becoming his disciple (Luke 14:26). Fundamental to the Christian ethic is the injunction to obey God rather than man (Acts 5:29). Before the Reformation only the celibate clergy and monastic orders were in theory expected to hearken to the injunction in its full severity. The Reformation radicalized and universalized the injunction by its doctrine of the priesthood of all believers. Without realizing it, the Reformers had unleashed the full revolutionary force of biblical religion's subordination of the natural sphere of human activity, namely, the nuclear family and the extended family we know as the nation, to a supramundane principle. However, the seeds of the subordination were already present in biblical Judaism. No commandment is more central to Jewish tradition and experience than that of honoring one's parents (Exod. 20:12; Deut. 5:16). Nevertheless, in Judaism filial piety is legitimated *ab extra* by the supramundane God who is the source of the commandments. When filial piety conflicts with obedience to God's commandments, the latter must take precedence, as is evident in the *Akedah* (Gen. 22:1-19). Ultimately, there is only one offense in biblical religion, namely, want of conformity with the will of God as expressed in the covenant between God and Israel.

In general, traditional societies can be understood as more or less autonomous, religiously-legitimated, extended kinship groups. In such groups far greater emphasis is accorded to collective than to individual interests. As we shall see, in spite of its modernization, Japan remains such a society. An enormous psychic effort is required to reject traditional society for the individualistic, depersonalized professionalism of the modern West. The effort may have involved the most radical value transformation in all of human history. Weber believed, correctly in my opinion, that only a religiously legitimate redefinition of the sacred could have fostered the transformation. The Reformation's assertion that all things human are to be subordinated to the sovereign Creator God gave Protestants the moral and emotional leverage with which to turn away from old ways and old authorities and to begin anew, not once but continually. It was psychologically possible for Luther to reject the authority of the pope in the name of God, as indeed he had rejected the authority of his own father when Hans vehemently opposed Martin's choice of a religious vocation; it would have been impossible for Luther to oppose the authority of either father on the basis of his personal authority alone. The modern world could only have come into being when it became possible for men to cast aside the emotional ties with which they were bound to the traditional order. This capacity to reject tradition became the source of the permanent revolution we call capitalism. As the German sociologist Wolfgang Schluchter has observed, "ascetic Protestantism . . . enabled a group of religious vertuosi . . . to overcome the psychological barriers which the guiding principles of personal loyalty put in the way of despersonalizing man's relation to the natural and social world."

By contrast, filial piety is at the heart of the Confucian ethic. Unlike biblical religion, the Confucian system has no point of leverage by means of which disobedience to parents could be justified. Without a willingness to breach the ethic of filial piety, as was done in Western religion, there does not seem to have been any way in which the revolutionary new beginnings necessary for modernization could have been initiated within a Confucian civilization.

Nevertheless, not only has East Asia modernized, but it has done so with far greater success than Africa, the Middle East, or Latin America. Moreover, if present trends continue, first Japan and then South Korea, Taiwan, Hong Kong, Singapore and, perhaps, the People's Republic of China are likely to outstrip Western Europe and the United States in economic development. Hence, the question arises whether Weber's Protestant-ethic hypothesis has been disproven. In reality, Weber did not hold that the non-Western nations were incapable of modernization. He did, however, believe that the process could only have been *initiated* in the Protestant West. Weber argued that the material factors necessary for capitalist development were at least as favorable in China and India as in the West. Since both East and West shared more or less comparable material conditions, these could not account for the difference in development. Weber found that difference in religion.[13]

Perhaps the most fundamental insight offered by Weber is that, in addition to appropriate material conditions, *traditional societies can only be transformed into modern societies by a radical redefinition of the sacred.*[14] The case of Japan would appear to confirm this insight. According to Marius B. Jensen, "The intellectual history of Japan in the first half of the nineteenth century is dominated by the consciousness of domestic weakness and foreign threat."[15] Even before the appearance of Commodore Matthew Perry and his "Black Ships" in 1853, word of China's 1842 humiliation at the hands of Great Britain had reached Japan. Shortly after China's defeat, a questionnaire was addressed by an official of the shogunate to one of the Hollanders living in Nagasaki. The European was asked, "Why have the Tartars lost, since they are said to be brave enough?" The Hollander replied, "Bravery alone is not sufficient, the art of war demands something more. No outlandish power can compete with a European one, as can be seen by the great realm of China which has been conquered by only four thousand men."[16] Given the Chinese foundation of much of Japanese civilization, China's defeat shocked many thoughtful Japanese. It was also an event that Japanese administrators could hardly ignore. When China's humiliation was followed by the forcible opening of Japan by Commodore Perry in 1853 and the unequal commercial treaties forced upon Japan between 1858 and 1866, Japan had the choice of either radically restructuring her society or suffering defeat and humiliation by the predatory Western powers. Moreover, Japan was threatened economically as well as militarily. The unequal treaties exposed Japan's pre-modern, agrarian economy to destructive competition on the part of the industrialized nations of the West. With tariffs on goods imported to Japan set by foreigners and with Japan's handicraft industries incapable of competing with Western factories, Japan soon found herself flooded with manufactured foreign goods that had the effect of ruining much of her domestic handicraft industries at a time when her currency was rapidly depreciating and high inflation was dangerously distorting her domestic economy.[17]

As we know, the foreign threat was met speedily and successfully by perhaps the most radical restructuring of any society the world has ever known. One of the most remarkable aspects of Japanese modernization is that it was carried out with relatively little bloodshed. The Samurai elite responsible for the Meiji Restoration of 1868 were genuine revolutionaries who had largely emerged out of a group of dissidents from the lower strata of their class. Crucial to the success of their revolution was the transformation wrought in the imperial office whose sacred charismatic character is deeply rooted in Japan's earliest history. Just as religion had played a crucial role in the modernization of the West, so, too, a very different kind of religion, one that rested upon the archaic institution of divine kingship played an equally important role in Japan's modernization.

For our purposes it will suffice to take brief note of the character of the imperial office in the *sengoku,* Tokugawa, and Meiji eras.[18] In the *sengoku jidai* period, the "period of the warring states" that preceded the Tokugawa shogunate, the emperors were often bitterly impoverished yet their office symbolized sacralized legitimate authority. The emperors were influential political rulers who could influence politics but could not rule. The Tokugawa shogunate brought to an end whatever overt political authority the emperors possessed. The shogun assumed almost all of the political prerogatives of the imperial office such as the bestowal of titles of nobility, the right to veto the appointment of court officials, and the right to govern those Buddhist monasteries formerly controlled by the imperial court. At the same time, the material conditions of the imperial court were greatly improved and the imperial office was treated with genuine reverence. Scholars responsible for formulating loyalist ideas concerning the throne in the late eighteenth century even discerned a causal connection between the Tokugawa shogunate's ability to pacify the country and its respectful attitude toward the emperor.[19] During this period, the emperor was the head of state and the shogun the functioning head of government.

It was fortunate for Japan that this division of authority existed in the period immediately preceding modernization. Had the supreme sovereign been the functioning head of government in the 1850s, his policies rather than the shogun's might have been discredited. As a result, there might not have been any institution to guarantee the continuity of legitimate authority from the pre-modern to the modern period and the Japanese would have been far less able to withstand the deterioration of their indigenous institutions in the face of the Western challenge. As it was, the period between 1860 and 1880 witnessed a tendency in Japan, by no means shared by all leaders, to overestimate Western culture and institutions and to denigrate their own indigenous institutions. It is also likely that Christianity would have made far greater inroads in Japan had the imperial office been discredited. We shall return to this question shortly.

The role of the monarchy changed in the Bakumatsu or late Tokugawa period. When it became apparent that the shogunate was unable to cope with the challenges confronting Japan, there were occasions on which expressions of political preference were enunciated in the name of the Emperor Komei, such as the refusal to ratify the treaty of 1858. However, even in this period, reverence to the throne did not normally involve direct imperial rule.

The final step in bringing the shogunate to an end was taken with the Meiji Restoration and the proclamation of the sacred character of the imperial office. The first article of the Constitution of 1889 reads: "The Empire of Japan shall be reigned over and governed by a line of Emperors unbroken for ages eternal." The third article reads: "The Emperor is sacred and inviolable." There is an element of vagueness in the third article that invites interpretation. Perhaps the most important interpreter of the Meiji era was Prince Ito who was largely responsible for drafting the written constitution. His *Commentaries on the Constitution* appeared in 1889 and his comment on the imperial office is instructive:

> The Sacred Throne was established at the time when the heavens and earth were separated. The Emperor is Heaven descended, divine and sacred; He is preeminent above all his subjects. He must be reverenced and is inviolable. He has indeed to pay due respect to the law, but the law has no power to hold him accountable to it. Not only shall there be no irreverence for the Emperor's person, but also He shall not be made a topic of derogatory comment nor one of discussion.[20]

As in the early Tokugawa period, the emperor's position was once again exalted. In addition, the policies of government were now depicted as representing the "Imperial will." At the same time, the emperor lost the ability to speak independently of his counselors. By transferring the emperor's residence from Kyoto to Edo, exalted though his position may have been, he spoke, if at all, through the oligarchs who governed in his name. No longer could dissidents claim to speak on his behalf in opposing the policies of government. The ceremonial aspects of the imperial institution were exalted, the emperor was effectively isolated from dissidents, and power was exercised in his name.

In spite of the loss of an active political role, the imperial institution gained an overwhelming new importance. As a direct descendant of the Sun Goddess Amaterasu-omi-kami, the emperor symbolized national continuity, identity, and sovereignty at a time when foreigners threatened these values more profoundly than at any other time in Japan's history. The emperor also symbolized national unity and the harmony between the rulers and the ruled. According to Herschel Webb, the Meiji oligarchs were thus able to utilize the imperial institution (a) "to give unprecedented policies the color of great antiquity" and (b) "to make it appear that what was in fact an administration by relatively lowly placed new men proceeded instead from the most highly pedigreed and unquestionably legitimate of all possible sources."[21]

When we compare the extreme social and political disorders that accompanied the transformation of traditional to modern societies in the Christian West with the relatively bloodless transformation that took place in non-Christian Japan, the Japanese achievement appears truly impressive. Unlike their modernizing counterparts in the English Revolution of the seventeenth century and the French Revolution of the late eighteenth century, who purchased the transformation of their respective societies with regicide and civil war, the modernizing elite of Japan succeeded in rationalizing the economy and society of their nation with a minimum of domestic violence or alienation of elite classes and institutions. By utilizing a seemingly conservative doctrine, that of the emperor's divinity, to legitimate a radical social and political revolution, the elite was able to create a strong central government, abolish all estate distinctions, eliminate warrior privileges, open military service to commoners hitherto forbidden to possess arms, establish a system of universal public education, and facilitate the entry of members of the samurai class, in general the best educated class, into the world of business and commerce. All this was done without the transformation of traditional elites and institutions into embittered enemies of the new social order as was so often the case in Europe. Modernization and political centralization were carried out under conditions of far greater social cohesiveness and stability than was the case elsewhere.

The doctrine of the emperor's divinity, his status as a "living kami," was crucial to the expeditious creation of a strong, centralized government, which could replace the shogunate, and establish an effective modern economy. By subordinating all other loyalties to loyalty to the emperor, the samurai were enabled to transfer their allegiance from local leaders, who in many cases could no longer support them, to the leader of the new centralized state and, perhaps of greater importance, to the oligarchs and bureaucrats who claimed to speak on his behalf. This was a precondition of successful modernization in an era of heavy industry requiring large-scale capital investment. Japanese modernization involved the blending of the most archaic traditions, albeit renovated under the pressure of new dangers, with the imperatives of economic, political and industrial rationalization.

We have already noted that a precondition of modernization in the West was the weakening of the value of filial piety. No such rejection was necessary for Japanese modernization. Apart from religion, filial piety had to be breached in the modernizing West in the relations between sovereign and subject. Normally, the Western "carriers" of modernization were the urbanized commercial classes rather than absolutist monarchs. The latter facilitated the modernization of the polity by the bureacratic rationalization of the state administration, but they were seldom inclined to set social hierarchies in disarray by favoring the urbanized carriers of modernization over the nobility whose roots were largely agrarian. Class warfare, often religiously legitimated, was an almost endemic by-product of Western modernization. By contrast, the social transformations necessary for modernization in Japan were initiated from the top down rather than from the middle up. Instead of abrogating filial piety, that value became an indispensable component of Japanese modernization.

That thoughtful Japanese leaders of the Meiji era were concerned lest too great a reliance on Western ways lead to the destruction of the value of filial piety is evident in the "Imperial Rescript: The Great Principles of Education, 1879," written by Motoda Eifu, the Confucian lecturer to the emperor. The rescript reads in part:

> Although we set out to take in the best features of the West and bring in new things in order to achieve the high aims of the Meiji restoration . . . this procedure had a serious defect: It reduced benevolence, justice, loyalty, and filial piety to a secondary position. The danger of indiscriminate emulation of Western ways is that in the end our people will forget the great principles governing the relations between ruler and subject, and father and son. Our aim, based on our ancestral teachings, is solely the clarification of benevolence, justice, loyalty, and filial piety.[22]

Men like Motoda saw the need for modernization. Nevertheless, they also understood one of the principal dangers of Western-style modernization, destruction of the historic continuity of Japanese civilization, and this the leaders of Japan were determined to resist. The Imperial Rescript on Education of 1890 gives expression to the determination of Japan's leaders to preserve the historic continuity of Japanese civilization and its values at a time of the most revolutionary socioeconomic transformations in all of Japanese history. Few, if any other documents, are as instructive in exhibiting the contrast between the Japanese and Western responses to modernization. Whereas the West initiated modernization with a rejection of the highest religious and political authorities, not excluding regicide, and tended to equate modernization with secularization, Japan undertook modernization under the authority of its supreme religio-political authority and in defense of the values of its traditional civilization. The document reads in part:

> Know ye, our Subjects!
>
> Our Imperial ancestors have founded our empire on a basis broad and everlasting and have deeply and firmly implanted virtue; our subjects, ever united in loyalty and filial piety, have from generation to generation illustrated the beauty thereof. This is the fundamental character of our empire, and herein also lies the source of our education. Ye, our subjects, be filial to your parents . . . pursue learning and cultivate arts, and thereby develop your intellectual facilities and perfect your moral powers; furthermore, advance the public good and promote common interests; always respect the constitution and observe the laws; *should any emergency arise, offer yourselves courageously to the state; and thus guard and maintain the prosperity of our Imperial throne, coeval with heaven and earth.* (italics added)[23]

The religious traditions fostering modernization in Japan and the West can thus be seen as polar opposites. Whether one is Jewish, Christian, or Moslem, it is impossible to worship the God of Abraham without rejecting the gods of one's earliest ancestors. When Joshua assembled the Israelite tribes at Schechem to swear fealty to the Lord, he reminded them: "Long ago your forefathers Terah and his sons Abraham and Nahor, lived beside the Euphrates and they worshipped other gods" (Joshua 24:2). *In order to worship the God of the Bible, somewhere in history a drastic uprooting process had to have taken place.* The old pagan gods had to be foresworn and the ways of one's oldest ancestors abandoned. This was as true of Moslems and Christians as it was of Jews. Here again, Catholicism sometimes mitigated the harshness of the process by identifying local deities with Christian saints. Not surprisingly, the young Hegel, although Lutheran by tradition, expressed his bitterness at this alienation from his own archaic religious inheritance:

Every nation has its own imagery, its gods, angels, devils or saints who live on in the nation's traditions . . . .

Christianity has emptied Valhalla, felled the sacred groves, extirpated the national imagery as a shameful superstition, as a devilish poison, and given us instead the imagery of a nation whose climate, laws, culture, and interests are strange to us and whose history has no connection whatever with our own. A David or a Solomon lives in our popular imagination, but our country's own heroes slumber in learned history books. . . .

Thus we are without any religious imagery which is homegrown or linked with our history . . . all that we have is the remains of an imagery of our own, lurking amid the common people under the name of superstition.

Hegel concluded his complaint by asking: "Is Judaea, then, the Teutons' fatherland?"[24]

The young Hegel understood the profoundly destabilizing character of the uprooting involved in the conversion of the Germans to biblical religion. He also appears to have grasped the fact that biblical religion is inherently uprooting, at least in the first generation. Biblical religion effectively begins when God commands Abram, "Get thee out of thine own country, and from thy kinsmen, and from thy father's house, and go unto a land that I will show you" (Gen. 12:1). It is instructive to recall the young Hegel's bitter condemnation of Abraham's voluntary uprooting:

Abram, born in Chaldea, had in youth already left a fatherland in his father's company. Now, in the plains of Mesopotamia, he tore himself free altogether from his family as well, in order to be a wholly self-subsistent, independent man, to be an overlord himself. He did this without having been injured or disowned, without the grief which after a wrong or an outrage signifies love's enduring need, when love, injured indeed but not lost, goes in quest of a new fatherland in order to flourish and enjoy itself there. The first act which made Abraham the progenitor of a nation is a disseverance which snaps the bonds of communal life and love. The entirety of the relationships in which he had hitherto lived with men and nature, these beautiful relationships of his youth (Joshua 24:2), he spurned.[25]

As noted, Abraham's departure from his native land entailed unconditional rejection of the gods of that land. And, all Jews, Christians, and Moslems are the heirs of their spiritual forefather's primal uprooting.

The contrast with earth-bound, non-nomadic Japan, a nation that has neither foresworn her most ancient gods nor thought of these spirits as separate from nature, could not be greater. Japan's modernization was predicated upon unconditional reaffirmation of the sacred connection between the modern state and its most archaic roots. One of National Socialism's long-range objectives was to eradicate the biblical heritage in Germany and regain Germany's archaic inheritance. The Japanese did not require the social and political violence inherent in the National Socialism to remain in touch with their roots. Unlike every nation of Judeo-Christian inheritance, the Japanese alone remain in contact with their oldest sources of religious and cultural values. Moreover, the Japanese have so structured their society and their economy that they will have no motive to abandon their most ancient traditions.

There are important similarities between the way the emperor functioned in Japanese society, at least until 1946, and the way the Pharaohs functioned in ancient Egypt. Both Japan and Egypt were sacralized kingdoms with dynasties of extremely long and stable duration. The following description of the role of the ancient Egyptian monarchy by Henri Frankfort is reminiscent of Prince Ito's comments concerning the emperor:

> The Egyptian state was not a man-made alternative to other forms of political organization. It was god-given, established when the world was created; and it continued to form part of the universal order. In the person of Pharaoh a superhuman being had taken charge of the affairs of man. And this great blessing, which ensured the well-being of the nation, was not due to a fortunate accident but had been foreseen in the divine plan. The monarchy then was as old as the world, for the creator himself had assumed kingly office on the day of creation. Pharaoh was his descendant and his successor.[26]

When in 1945 the victorious Americans used their political leverage to secure the emperor's denial of his divinity, they were responding to the institution of divine kingship in a way that accorded with their age-old biblical tradition. Because of the cultural predominance of sectarian Protestantism in the United States and the absence of a feudal inheritance, American culture has been more strongly influenced by biblical religion than any other Western country. According to William P. Woodard, who served as an advisor on religion to General Douglas MacArthur's occupation administration, the general was conscious of being called by the biblical God for the hour, and regarded himself as the leader of the Protestant world "as the Pope was the leader of the Catholic world."[27] Although the general later moderated the tone of his remarks, in the early years of the occupation, MacArthur made unfavorable comments about both Buddhism and Shinto.[28] He favored the return of Christian missionaries in large numbers to Japan and saw the occupation as an unparalleled opportunity for the conversion of the Japanese to Christianity.[29] MacArthur saw himself as called by the God of the Bible to lead the Japanese out of what he, as a believing Christian, regarded as their spiritual ignorance.

In spite of apparently favorable circumstances, the post-war missionaries who came to Japan quickly discovered that few, if any, free countries offer less promise to Christian missions that Japan. After more than a century of strenuous efforts, with one of the world's largest concentrations of foreign missionaries, almost 5,200 in number, Japan remains more resistant to Christianity than any other developed country. Less than one per cent of the population is Christian and the numbers are declining.[30] By contrast, many observers anticipate that neighboring South Korea, whose Christian population comprises almost 25 percent of the whole, will have a Christian majority by the year 2000.[31] Apart from the fact that Christianity is rejected as "unJapanese" by a population with a very strong sense of group identity and a strong distrust of anything foreign that cannot be readily assimilated, the Japanese find the biblical conceptions of an omnipotent, extramundane Creator who establishes a covenant with a non-Japanese group utterly lacking in credibility. The Japanese believe themselves to be descendants of a race of gods and their emperor a direct descendant of the Sun Goddess, but, as we have seen, descent is an organic rather than a conditional relationship as in the case of the convenantal relationship with the transcendent Creator God.

Another respect in which the paths to modernization taken by Japan and the United States have been profoundly different has been the "disenchantment of the world." As noted above, biblical monotheism, with its affirmation of one sovereign Creator God and its persistent tendency to desacralize both the natural and political orders, led to the "disenchantment," that is, the rejection of animism, polytheism, and magic in the civilizations that derived from biblical religion. Contemporary sociologists of religion tend to concur in Weber's judgment that biblical "disenchantment of the world" was an indispensable precondition of the rationalization of the economy and society characteristic of Western capitalism.[31] It is precisely that which a "disenchanting" religion rejects, namely, animism and polytheism, that Shinto affirms. Here again, indigenous Japanese religion is the polar opposite of the biblical tradition. Moreover, although we cannot go into detail, it should be noted that, in spite of its animism and polytheism, Shinto plays a significant role in contemporary Japanese business, science, and technology. For example among the leading corporations that have Shinto shrines at their headquarters, branches, and industrial establishments are the Sanwa Group, Toyota, the Mitsubishi Group, Hitachi, Toshiba, and Matsushita. Konosuke Matsushita, founder of the giant Matsushita Electric Company (Panasonic, Quasar) and one of this century's preeminent Japanese business leaders, has served for many years as president of the Worshippers of Ise Shrine, Japan's most sacred shrine.[33] Groundbreaking ceremonies for new factories usually involve a Shinto ritual, as was the case at the groundbreaking ceremonies for Mazda's new automobile factory in Michigan and the jointly-owned Chrysler-Mitsubishi American factory. The governor of Michigan was in attendance at the two-hour ceremony for the Mazda factory.

Biblical religion and indigenous Japanese religious tradition have thus provided alternative paths to the modern world. Biblical religion alone, with its denigration of filial piety and its tradition of relativizing human institutions in the light of the ideal of service to a sovereign Creator God, possessed the psychic mechanism to begin the monumental breach with the past implied in modernization. It alone had a value system that legitimated the break with the past as service to an ultimate principal. Furthermore, by eliminating the necessity to appease any spirits or divinities thought to inhere in the natural or political order, biblical "disenchantment" fostered the functional rationality in finance, scientific experimentation, bureaucratic organization, and the processes of production, which was indispensable to the creation of the bourgeois capitalist world.[34] One can without exaggeration say that the modern Western world is largely an unintended consequence of the cultural triumph of a biblical understanding of the nature of things.

Nevertheless, if Japan did not have a value system capable of initiating a fundamental breach with the past, it did have the religious and cultural resources necessary to *defend* its civilization against the West. And, that it has done with astonishing success. As noted, *modernization in Japan was essentially a defensive strategy*. Its first objective was to secure Japan against Western military aggression, its second was to defend Japan against Western economic aggression. Its ultimate purpose was to defend Japanese civilization against the destruction of its historic values, which would most assuredly have ensued if Japan as a nation had been converted to any form of biblical religion. Japan would have been compelled to abandon the gods and ways of its ancestors as surely as had Abraham's progeny in Judaism, Christianity, and Islam.

If Japan is not yet the world's richest nation, it soon will be. Its extraordinary achievements have a meaning, both for Japan and the world, which transcends economic success. There is, for example, the question of whether Japan will become the world's number one military superpower in the twenty-first century. I have discussed that issue elsewhere.[35] Here, we are interested in the cultural and religious rather than the possible military consequences of the Japanese "miracle." One consequence is already apparent. The majority of Japanese have interpreted their post-war economic and technological achievements as confirming the superiority of their civilization over that of their trading partners and competitors. If ever the Japanese were amenable to conversion to a biblical religion, that time has past. Recently, the prime minister's office published a translation of a dialogue between then Prime Minister Yasuhiro Nakasone and Professor Takeshi Umehara, one of his country's leading Japanologists. In the course of the dialogue, the prime minister offered the following comment on Japanese religion:

> The Japanese tend toward polytheism rather then monotheism. We believe in many Gods and consider ourselves part of nature's unending cycle. There is broad and general acceptance of the idea that man's fate is inseparable from that of every animal, tree, and blade of grass.
>
> Side by side with this is the Indian concept that each man is the whole of nature unto himself—as is evident in Zen philosophy as well. The Japanese combine both of these concepts, oneness with nature and the individual as the whole of nature, within their being. It is my belief, however, that our sense of oneness with nature is indigenous and goes back to our Jomon roots. Japan's ancestor worship is thus quite different from Christianity's contract between man and his monotheistic god. In the process of honoring our forefathers, we create the harmony which is such an integral part of our lifestyle.[36]

According to Umehara, Japan's "Jomon roots" cover a period that preceded the introduction of agriculture and lasted almost 10,000 years, coming to an end about 300 B.C.E. The prime minister thus asserts that Japan's religious culture goes back to her earliest roots. This is not a heritage he or any other Japanese is likely to abandon. Nor do all Japanese regard the emperor's post-war denial of his divinity as having really changed his "divine" status. In a document prepared for the Ninth International Congress for the History of Religions (1958), the Shinto Publications Committee declared:

> Since the change was merely a change in outward treatment, it is only natural that the Shinto of the Imperial House and Shrine Shinto should still be considered orthodox. It is one of the noteworthy peculiarities of Shinto as a religion that, since these types of Shinto are not bound by dogmas and scriptures but preserve their life in traditional form, in so long as there is no great impediment in the continuation of the religious rituals, the wounds inflicted by this change are not too deep.[37]

The "divinity" of the emperor was never considered comparable to that of Jesus in Christianity of God in biblical Judaism. The emperor was thought of as *ikigami,* "a living human kami." The term refers to outstanding servants of the nation who might be enshrined and worshipped while still alive. Imperial princes, national heroes, Shinto priests and the emperor can all be reverenced as *ikigami*. To the Japanese, the emperor remains the supreme living kami. At present, his status is somewhat ambiguous. As Japan's power continues to grow, there is every likelihood that the ambiguity will be clarified in favor of the traditional understanding of the emperor's "divine" status.

Unlike most allegedly "primitive" indigenous religions, Japanese religion has demonstrated its power to inspire a civilization capable of competing successfully with the West in almost every significant sphere of human activity. Seldom, if ever, has the monotheistic exclusivism of biblical religion been challenged as successfully as it has by modern Japan.

It should be obvious that I have profound respect for the achievements of Japanese civilization, especially in the Meiji and post-World War II periods. Nevertheless, I feel constrained to conclude by raising an issue that may prove to be of considerable importance in the years ahead. Those who fault biblical religion for its exclusivism tend to overlook one of its principal strengths, namely, its ability to unite men and women hitherto strangers to each other in a new community of worship and moral obligation. Indeed, the covenant at Sinai served that function when it transformed a "mixed multitude" of escaped fugitives into a community united in worship of the God who redeemed them from Egypt. Enlarging on an impulse already present in Scripture, Christianity was able to create a community of moral obligation which transcended old religio-communal boundaries of ethnicity and common descent.[38] It is perhaps no accident that the United States is both the modern nation most committed to biblical religion and to the absorption of an immigrant population of every race, color, and creed. If, as Ben-Dasan asserts, the relation between Israel and God is "artificial" rather than organic, the bonds the founding fathers created to unite Americans were also a matter of human invention, losing none of their potency thereby. By contrast, while Japan has been most successful in defending the integrity, continuity, and organic character of its civilization, its indigenous traditions offer little basis for a wider base of community than that which rests on kinship and common descent. Apart from the obvious constraints Japan's limited space imposes upon the size of her population, Japan is, of all modern nations, the least able culturally and psychologically to absorb new immigrants, even in the case of Koreans, who are often physically indistinguishable from Japanese. Here again, Japan and the United States are polar opposites.

In view of the overwhelming international importance of Japan, one must ask whether she can any longer ignore the problem of finding a more universal basis for community than is offered by her indigenous traditions. Were Japan a minor provincial power, this issue might be of little consequence. However, Japan is not a minor power but a world leader and there is a profound conflict between the traditions that have enabled Japan to achieve her current position and the universal responsibilities that that position demands. Whatever shortcomings can be discerned in biblical religion, it has repeatedly demonstrated its capacity to enlarge humanity's sense of community. The question of whether Japan has the indigenous spiritual resources to enlarge her sense of community may be the most important issues confronting her in the coming Pacific era.

NOTES

1. This assessment of the relationship between biblical religion and the secular spirit rests upon the view that it has been the destiny of biblical religion to negate itself in ever-widening domains of human activity. See Peter Berger, *The Sacred Canopy: Elements of a Sociological Theory of Religion* (Garden City: Anchor books, 1969), pp. 105-126. However, long before contemporary sociologists of religion came to interpret the secularization process as a dialectical consequence of Christianity, the

secular consciousness was thus understood by Hegel and a number of nineteenth-century German philosophical critics of the Christian religion. Karl Löwith has observed: "Philosophical criticism of the Christian religion began in the nineteenth century and reached its climax with Neitzsche. It is a Protestant movement, and therefore specifically German. This holds true both of the criticism and the religion at which it was directed. Our critical philosophers were all theologically educated Protestants, and their criticism of Christianity presupposes its Protestant manifestations." Löwith, *From Hegel to Nietzsche: The Revolution in Nineteenth-Century Thought* (New York: Holt, Rhinehart and Winston, 1964), p. 327. According to Löwith, Hegel "translates" the forms of religion, which belong to the imagination, into the conceptualization of reason. Löwith observes that "the historical consequence of Hegel's ambigous 'translation' was an absolute destruction of Christian philosophy and of the Christian religion," a development that became fully manifest in the work of Friedrich Nietzsche. *From Hegel to Nietzsche,* p. 333.

2. The Weber hypothesis was first stated in Max Weber, *The Protestant Ethic and the Spirit of Capitalism,* (1904) trans. Talcott Parsons (New York: Charles Scribner's Sons, 1958). The Parsons translation is of the revised version of the essay published in Weber, *Gesammelte Aufsätze zur Religionssoziologie* (Tübingen: J. C. B. Mohr, 1920).

3. Weber, *Protestant Ethic,* p. 104.

4. On the sanctioning of the taking of interest, see Benjamin Nelson, *The Idea of Usury: from Tribal Brotherhood to Universal Otherhood* (Chicago: University of Chicago Press, 1969), pp. 73-83.

5. Max Weber, "Science as a Vocation" on H. H. Gerth and C. Wright Mills, *From Max Weber: Essays in Sociology* (New York: Oxford University Press, 1946), p. 139.

6. See Peter Berger, *The Sacred Canopy: Elements of a Sociological Theory of Religion* (Garden City: Anchor Books, 1969), pp. 111-125.

7. See article, "Covenant" in *Encyclopedia Judaica* (Jerusalem: 1972), V, pp. 1012-1022 and George Mendenhall, *The Tenth Generation: The Origins of the Biblical Tradition* (Baltimore: Johns Hopkins University Press, 1973), pp. 64-66.

8. Robert Bellah, "Father and Son in Christianity and Confucianism" in Bellah, *Beyond Belief: Essays on Religion in a Post Traditional World* (New York: Harper and Row, 1970), pp. 76-99.

9. Article, "Covenant" in *Encyclopedia Judaica.*

10. Isaiah ben-Dasan, *The Japanese and the Jews,* trans. Richard L. Gage (Tokyo: Weatherhill, 1985), pp. 134 ff.

11. For a discussion of the subordination of the natural family to the imperatives of faith in Pauline Christianity, see Richard L. Rubenstein, *My Brother Paul* (New York: Harper and Row, 1972), pp. 54-77.

12. Wolfgang Schluchter, *The Rise of Western Rationalism: Max Weber's Developmental History,* trans. Guenther Roth (Berkeley: University of California Press, 1981), p. 173.

13. See Talcott Parsons, *The Structure of Social Action: A Study in Social Theory with Special Reference to a Group of Recent European Writers,* Vol. II (New York: Free Press, 1968), pp. 539-578.

14. See Robert Bellah, *Tokugawa Religion: The Values of Pre-Industrial Japan*

(Glencoe, Ill.: The Free Press, 1957), p. 8.

15. Marius Bl Jensen, "Changing Japanese Attitudes Toward Modernization," in Marius B. Jensen, ed., *Changing Japanese Attitudes Toward Modernization* (Princeton: Princeton University Press, 1965), p. 54.

16. C. R. Boxer, *Jan Compagnie in Japan* (The Hague, 1950), App. v, pp. 185-187. Cited by Jensen, *op. cit.,* p. 57.

17. See T. C. Smith, *Political Change and Industrial Development in Japan* (Stanford: Stanford University Press, 1955), pp. 25-41.

18. For an informed analysis of the transformations in the role of the emperor from the period known as *sengoku jidai* "the period of the warring states," through the Tokugawa, Bakumatsu, and Meiji eras, see Herschel Webb, "The Development of an Orthodox Attitude Toward the Imperial Institution in the Nineteenth Century," in Jensen, *op. cit.*

19. For example, Fujita Yukoku (1774-1826) wrote, "What qualities enable the shogunate to unite the country? Above, its reverent attitude toward the emperor, and below, its protective treatment of the feudal lords. Its rule, however, is nothing more than the exercise of the emperor's sovereignty. . . ." Kikuchi Kenjiro, ed., *Yukoku zenshu* (Tokyo: 1935), p. 229, cited by Webb, *op. cit.,* p. 177.

20. Hirobumi Ito, *Commentaries on the Constitution of the Empire of Japan* (Tokyo: Government Printing House, 1899) trans. Miyoji Ito, cited by D. C. Holtom, *Modern Japan and Shinto Nationalism* (Chicago: University of Chicago Press, 1947), p. 9.

21. Webb, *op. cit.,* p. 167.

22. "Imperial Rescript: The Great Principles of Education, 1879" in John Livingston, et. al. eds., *The Japan Reader: Imperial Japan: 1800-1945* (New York: Pantheon Books, 1973), p. 150.

23. "Imperial Rescript on Education, 1890" in Livingston, *op. cit.*

24. G. W. F. Hegel, "The Positivity of Christianity" in Hegel, *Early Theological Writings,* trans. T. M. Knox (Chicago: University of Chicago Press: 1948), pp. 145-148.

25. Hegel, "The Spirit of Christianity and its Fate" in *Early Theological Writings,* pp. 185-186.

26. Henri Frankfort, *Ancient Egyptian Religion* (New York: Columbia University Press, 1948), pp. 30-31.

27. William P. Woodard, *The Allied Occupation of Japan 1945-1952 and Japanese Religions* (Leiden: E. J. Brill, 1972), p. 241.

28. Woodard, *op. cit,* pp. 241-245.

29. Douglas MacArthur, Letter to Dr. Louis D. Newton of Atlanta, December 13, 1945. Cited by Woodard, *op. cit.,* p. 244.

30. Bernard Wysocki, Jr., "Christian Missions Convert Few in Japan," *Asian Wall Street Journal* (July 16, 1978).

31. See cover story, "Korea: The Cross as Catalyst," *Far Eastern Economic Review,* (April 19, 1984): 44-54.

32. See, for example, Berger, *op. cit.,* pp. 105-125.

33. Honda Soichiro, "Shinto in Japanese Culture," *Nanzan Bulletin,* No. 8/1984, pp. 24-30. (The *Bulletin* is published by Nanzan Institute of Religion and Culture, Nanzan University, Nagoya, Japan). This article originally appeared in Japanese as

"Bunka no naka no Shinto," in *Shukyo Shinbun,* February 1 and March 1, 1984. Honda Soichiro is the founder of the Honda Motor Company.

34. See Richard L. Rubenstein, *The Age of Triage* (Boston: Beacon Press, 1983), pp. 2ff; David Landes, *The Unbound Prometheus: Technological Change and Industrial Development in Western Europe from 1750 to the Present* (Cambridge: Cambridge University Press, 1969), pp. 21-24.

35. See Richard L. Rubenstein, "Will Japan Be the World's No. 1 Superpower in the 21st Century?" in *The Academician* (Tokyo) vol. 3, no. 3/4 (Autumn/Winter, 1985): 14-18.

36. "The Flow of World Civilization and Japan's Role in the 21st Century: A Dialogue between Prime Minister Yasuhiro Nakasone and Professor Takeshi Umehara," Tokyo: Prime Minister's Office (April 1986): 11. I am indebted to Dr. John Tepper Marlin of New York City for this reference.

37. Cited in stuart D. B. Picken, *Shinto: Japan's Spiritual Roots* (Tokyo: Kodansha, 1980), p. 40.

38. This point has been made effectively by Fustel de Coulanges, *The Ancient City: A Study on the Religion, Laws, and Institutions of Greece and Rome* (1864) (Garden City: Doubleday Anchor Books, 1956), pp. 389-396.

13

Religion and the Debasement of Goodness

Richard Taylor

Most humanists who share my aversion to the Christian religion are athiests, but they nevertheless praise the ethical ideals that they associate with Christianity, particularly those attaching great value to being human. Christians declare every human being to be precious, to have been created in the very image of God, the lowliest among us thus being every bit as good as the greatest and noblest. And humanists, while avoiding the theological language of this declaration, nevertheless affirm the same thing. Indeed, it is common for humanists to criticize Christians, not for their ethical ideals, but for their failure to live up to them. We humanists, they say in effect, carry the ideals of Christianity into our practice better than Christians themselves. There is sometimes much truth in this, but the point I am making is that those ethical ideals themselves are not subjected to doubt or serious criticism. It is, rather, the theological claims that are scorned and, most emphatically, belief in any god.

Let it be clear at the outset, then, that my position is rather opposite to that of humanists on both points. I do, most emphatically, believe in God, and I just as emphatically reject the ethic of Christianity, which appears to me to be the corruption and debasement of what is truly noble. By God I mean the creator of heaven and earth, and of all things visible and invisible; God's reality is to me as obvious as my own. This is the language of the creeds, and on this point I have no quarrel with Christians. I consider the details of Christian theology,

Richard Taylor is professor emeritus of philosophy at the University of Rochester and Levitt-Spencer Professor of Philosophy at Union College.

particularly those concerning the nature and role of its founder, to be laughably absurd, to be sure, but it is not part of my purpose to go into that. I want, instead, to cast doubt on the ethical ideas embodied in Christianity. Though these ideas are almost universally praised in our democratic culture, and even sometimes thought of as its very foundation, I believe that they are not merely wretched and stupid, but the perversion of what a genuinely noble ethical ideal should be.

Let me, then, begin by introducing a principle that seems so general that I shall call it a law and give it a name. I shall call it the *law of epigony*. The term derives from Greek mythology, the Epigones having been a group of rulers who, in trying to carry out the great principles of their predecessors, managed to debase and corrupt them. An epigone is thus an inferior imitator, an heir to something noble, who, in his defense of it, corrupts it. And what I have in mind by what I call the *law* of epigony is this: That *everything* that is originally truly noble and good comes to be corrupted by the very human beings whose mission it is to protect and preserve it, and that this corruption takes the form of substituting for what is noble and good something worthless, which is then extolled in its place.

What the principle asserts, then, and what is important to note, is that things noble and good tend to be weakened and debased, not by those who attack them, but by their very defenders. The great destroyer is not he who is bent on destroying. It is the human touch itself that corrupts.

That is the first idea that my law is intended to express. And the second part of my law expresses the manner of such corruption, namely, the substitution of some worthless thing, and the veneration of it.

I believe that religions all over the world exemplify this law as soon as they become settled and accepted and when anything resembling a priesthood arises within them. But before leaping to that point it will be useful to illustrate my law with commonplace examples. Many things would serve for this, but I shall illustrate the law first with the concepts of patriotism and marriage. Then I shall consider religion and, finally, the effect of popular religion upon ethics.

EPIGONY AND THE DEBASEMENT OF PATRIOTISM

Patriotism, as we all know, means the love for one's country. This is quite a simple idea, easily grasped. And since the love for anything good is itself something good, it is easy to see why it is considered an imperative to nourish such patriotism, especially in the hearts of the young—always provided, of course, that one's country, its institutions, and ideals are truly noble. That is the original meaning of patriotism. But what does it come to mean in fact? It comes to mean the love, not for one's country, but for the *symbols* of one's country, symbols that are in themselves worthless and even, sometimes, pernicious. Thus our image of the patriot is of someone who venerates a *flag,* which is in itself nothing but a garish piece of cloth and the paradigm of a mere symbol. The patriot's treatment of this symbolic object becomes ritualized to the extreme. Rules govern the times and manner in which it is displayed, how it is to be treated when not in use, even the manner of folding it up and, eventually, disposing of it when it has become tattered. He is incensed if the flag is flown upside down, used as a mop, or otherwise defiled. It is as though it were *itself* the object of the patriot's love—which, indeed, it has become.

Other mere symbols of the love of country come to fill the same surrogate role, such as, for example, certain recitals, anthems, and pledges; certain dates, particularly those marking the anniversaries of great military victories; certain garb, especially that associated with soldiering; and certain monuments, such as those erected to illustrious military figures, or the colossal Liberty statue that stands in the New York harbor, and so on. And what needs to be emphasized is that the thing all such symbols stand for recedes to invisibility, the symbols themselves taking its place as objects of veneration. Thus things that are indeed totally worthless, except as symbolizing some truly noble thing, come to be invested with an imagined worth of their own. This might be harmless enough, except for the fact that what *is* truly noble and good, the great thing or idea originally symbolized, is lost sight of altogether. And all this is done in the very name of what has, in effect, been cast aside.

The working of my law was quite dramatically illustrated recently in connection with the celebrations surrounding the Liberty statue. Much was made of the statue itself, millions of dollars were spent in polishing it up, throngs gathering to behold it, and so on. But virtually no thought was given to what it was originally supposed to symbolize. Some of the efforts of the news media in this direction were grotesque in their vulgarity. For example, people watching these celebrations on television were at one point shown a gathering of the wealthy who had paid five thousand dollars each for a choice spot to dine and look at the statue.

Some of these were interviewed, as somehow fulfilling the statue's symbolic meaning, the astonishing supposition being that it represented the freedom to come to these shores and make money. Indeed, the expression "the American dream" was repeatedly used to mean precisely that.

Similarly, in connection with these same celebrations, the *word* "liberty" was much used—in fact it was woven into every speech and exultation—but at no point did anyone actually stop to consider what that word is supposed to mean. The *word itself,* which is but a symbol of a precious and noble idea, came to be the thing that was prized, rather than the fairly clear and definite idea that it once symbolized. And what is so sad about all this is that virtually no one noticed the immense perversion that had been wrought. Imagining themselves to be giving expression to the sense and feelings of patriotism—that is, the love for one's country and certain of its noble ideas and institutions— people instead indulged gross and vulgar sentiments for the mere symbols of these, without any awareness of the corruption they were thus fostering.

EPIGONY AND THE DEBASEMENT OF MARRIAGE

The second familiar thing I will use to illustrate my law is the institution of marriage, something as familiar and commonplace as patriotism. The marriage of a man and woman is supposed to rest for its foundation upon their love for each other. Such love being genuine and over- whelming, it is rightly assumed that it will endure, and that the marriage built upon it will also endure. The perfectly human act of "getting" married is thus supposed to be a symbolic recognition of what already exists, namely, intense, indestructible, and binding love. It is, accordingly, this love that is supposed to unite its partners, not the man-made and symbolic recognition of such love. This is, indeed, more or less recognized in the Roman Catholic Church, where marriage is treated as a sacrament whose vehicle is considered to be, not a priest, but the lovers themselves. It is they who formally marry each other. Yet in popular thinking the very opposite is thought to be true, for everyone imagines that it is some clerk, religious or secular—that is, some priest or judge—who thus brings two people together in marriage and who "makes" them, as it is imagined, "really married."

This debasement of marriage at the hands of its most solemn de- fenders is particularly illustrative of my law. They substitute a legalistic form for the conjugal love that the form symbolizes. Thus they find no absurdity in the supposition that a man and woman might be married even though they have come to detest each other, their marital state having been established once for all at a stroke. Not surprisingly, they have great difficulty in seeing how a real marriage can exist without the legalistic act, no matter how overwhelming and indestructible might be the love that unites its partners. That, in other words, which one would have supposed was merely symbolic of something inexpressibly precious has preempted the thing symbolized. There are, doubtless, important practical reasons for this, but the fact remains that something good and noble is thereby debased by the very persons who imagine that they are upholding it. The defenders of what is good become, again, insidious destroyers, quite unwittingly.

Similarly, one sometimes finds the institution of marriage described as a form of *contract,* and, amazingly, those who put forth this wretched notion imagine that they are expressing a high standard. Indeed, they are apt to express this idea with moralistic fervor. Infidelity is thus represented as a kind of breach of contract, an act of promise-breaking, and is regarded as wrong for *that* reason. The bond of marriage, which was originally precious love, is thus replaced by the most vulgar kind of bond imaginable, upon which business transactions are supposed to rest. And note once again that this substitution of the worthless for that which was truly good is made by the very defenders of marriage. Having lost sight of what it really is, they uphold instead a worthless symbol of what it is supposed to be.

Of course the marriage of a man and a woman does involve a basic promise, namely, the promise to love. But the evil of the failure to love, or of the erosion of that love over time, is not that some promise has been broken. It is, rather, that something precious beyond words— that love itself—has been lost. It is doubtless important that lovers should not lie to each other. But no ultimate good is attained merely by heeding that precept, important as it may be. The ultimate good is that they should love each other, and for that reason have no incentive to lie or betray, or even to contemplate it. Yet it is common to find partners in a marriage, whose bond of love has long since diminished almost to zero, taking satisfaction in themselves, and being praised by others for having kept to their vows, stuck it out, and made it last. Perhaps there is something admirable in this, as a feat of endurance, but it is not any worthwhile concept of marriage that has been sustained. The very opposite has happened, and in perfect accordance with my law.

EPIGONY AND THE DEBASEMENT OF RELIGION

The third illustration of my law is found in the course that religions everywhere take as soon as any kind of priesthood is established, or, in other words, as soon as human defenders of any religion come forward. The priests themselves become the epigones, the vulgarizers of what was noble and good, and this corruption of the good is wrought, again, in the very name of that good. My law seems to hold no matter whether we are referring to religion as it is expressed in Islam, Buddhism, Christianity, or whatever.

Thus, as patriotism is originally the love for one's country, and marriage is originally the love of its partners for each other, so religion is originally the love for one god or many gods. This surely is its underlying meaning. It is this love that inspires the Bible, for instance, and from this that we draw our own inspiration in the study of sacred writings. It is what is absolutely essential to the mind and heart of a religious person. Mere belief in the *existence* of gods can have no more significance to religion than belief in the existence of anything else. Thus, to draw again from my two earlier examples, a person is not made a patriot by merely believing that his country exists, but by his love for it. A marriage is not made by each partner acknowledging that the other exists, but by their love for each other. So, too, for our creator. And this is why the Greeks of antiquity, despite their robust belief in the gods, were nevertheless hardly religious at all. The gods inspired in them fear and awe, but not the love that is inseparable from religion. On the other hand, every expression of a profound love for God, whether in word or deed, is instantly seen as religious, no matter what beliefs or speculations may or may not accompany it. Belief *in* God involves a great deal more than an ontological hypothesis, however firmly held, that there *is* a god.

But what happens when human beings organize to uphold and defend religion? Exactly what, by my law of epigony, we should expect; namely, the *symbols* of religion come to be the things venerated, to the extent that our creator, who was the original object of love in the heart of the religious, is entirely eclipsed by them. And, since religions are always rich in symbolism, the possibilities and the temptations for such substitution are quite overwhelming.

Thus, persons are thought of as religious if they exhibit great devotion to a *church:* attend its services regularly, give to it, and make it more or less central to their life's activities. Indeed, in the minds of the extremely vulgar, being religious is virtually equated with "going" to church. Religion, however, is the love for God, not the love for an institution, no matter how old, venerable, and powerful that institution may be. Hence, devotion to a church, instead of being the mark of a religious person, is the mark of one who is not religious at all, except in a debased and popular sense.

Similarly, many persons imagine themselves to express profound religiosity by their submission to a priesthood, or to certain of its exalted members, such as a bishop, an ayatollah or a grand lama. Indeed, this is, for reasons not hard to understand, fostered by the priesthood itself, apparently with no awareness that religion is thereby debased. The epigones, whose very role is the defense of religion, become its most insidious destroyers, setting before the faithful such things as holy books; holy personages; various objects and vestments; ceremonious behavior, sometimes on a grand scale; meaningless relics and bones of holy personages and things; and encouraging the veneration of these. In reducing what may once have been a believer, possessed with a heart and mind of love for God, to one who submits to a church and its priesthood, bowing to these, embracing their teachings, and submitting to their laws, a priesthood replaces religion with something quite different and quite vulgar—all too unwittingly. So again, the destroyers of what was truly noble and good turn out to be, not its avowed enemies, but its most dedicated human defenders. It is, as in the case of all things good, the human touch itself that corrupts in the very act of trying to foster and preserve. What makes the process more pathetic is the lack of realization that something very precious has been lost and something commonplace has been exalted. The destroyers of religion actually think of themselves as its upholders and defenders, and in this there is very often no insincerity. A bishop who ceaselessly dedicates himself to his church and its role in human affairs certainly does not think of himself as a foe of religion, but the very opposite, and in this he is perfectly sincere. The illusion is completed when his followers, heeding his exhortations, think of themselves, and of him, as religious. It is the final irony, and a profoundly sad one.

It is the working of this law that seems to me to explain many commonplace things having to do with the church and the clergy. For example, the only president of the United States who was driven from office by his own venality and corruption had, shortly before, been named Churchman of the Year. It was devotion to *church* that was thought to matter or, worse, the mere appearance of this, without even any thought concerning what may or may not lie behind it. The symbol had replaced the thing symbolized. Similarly, I once heard a Roman Catholic priest express concern that one of his parishioners might marry a Protestant, saying to her: "You see, we (*sic*) might lose not only you, but your children as well." This is one of those common and even banal examples of how, in keeping with my law, the corruption of something good is wrought, as in this case, by one of its official defenders. Or again, when Pope John Paul appeared, of all places, on the plains of Iowa a few years ago, he was surrounded by a vast sea of people who had come to see *him*. His very vestments—which, it might be noted, always come to clothe anyone deemed somehow "holy" in the public imagination—bespeak the power of symbolism, and also its destructiveness.

The workings of my law are found no less in the sometimes grotesque behavior of evangelical clergymen, their influence over the masses and their power to extract staggering amounts of money from the faithful for the furtherance of purely temporal causes. Here the debasement of what is sacred achieves a new dimension as these epigones convert the love of God to, of all things, the love of *self,* and religion is reduced to narcissism. Their followers, bathing themselves in self-glorification, declare *themselves* to be, above all, moral, patriotic, and blessed. Their faces radiant with happiness, they go forth, Bibles in hand, to make everyone else like themselves in the cause of religion.

How far the love of God is driven from religion by the human touch is indicated by the fact that what passes for religion is sometimes compatible with no belief in God at all. Thus a Jewish friend of mine, planning to marry a gentile, tried to reassure his mother by saying that it was in no sense a "mixed" marriage, because they were in total agreement on all theological matters, both being atheists; to which his mother responded, "Well, I don't see why you couldn't marry a *Jewish* athiest." One cannot fail to see that this woman's remark, though mildly amusing, has a point. Modern Judaism, though still considered one of the world's religions, is in fact little more than a culture. What is required, in order to be a Jew, is not a love for God, or even belief that any gods exist. All that is required is Jewish parentage, or in other words, a certain cultural identity.

It would not be so easy to speak of a Christian atheist without a sense of contradiction, and yet something like this is not uncommon. Thus, for example, a person born of Roman Catholic parents and baptized in that church might go through his entire life giving no real thought whatever to his creator. So long as he called himself a Roman Catholic, however, and went to mass and to confession with a certain minimum regularity—perhaps once a year—then his claim to be a Roman Catholic would not be challenged. Here what counts is not cultural identity but allegiance to a church, and even this need not be strong. In cases where the allegiance is very strong one hears applied the expression, "a good Catholic." What is meant here is that the person so described heeds the practices and laws of the church, particularly those requiring participation in its rituals. It does *not* mean that his heart is filled with a love for God, though this is somehow assumed to be implied. Of course it need not even be implied, for it would be perfectly possible for one to be a very "good Catholic" with only the minimal thought, from one day to another, of God, and with no genuine love for God at all.

Indeed, to make my point in still another way, it is customary to think of children, and even infants, as possessed of religion. This idea is absurd in its very nature, and yet it is absolutely insisted upon and even enforced by law. Thus an infant born of a Jewish woman must be adopted by persons "of the same religion," and the same holds for Catholic and Protestant babies—as if there were any theological sense in which an infant could, for example, be a Protestant. Religion is here considered a cultural identity and nothing more.

It will perhaps be said, very plausibly, that this humanization of things noble and good is necessary, given the inherent limitation of human beings, and that it is not therefore to be condemned. We cannot all of us be like St. Francis of Assisi. We are imperfect people living in an imperfect world, but live there we must, making the best we can of what we have.

This is of course true, but it misses the point. I have not said that everything should be perfect. I have not said that if such things as patriotism, marriage, and religion cannot be what they should be, then they should be abolished altogether. What I have said is that such things, which are in their true nature noble and good, always come to be corrupted by their upholders, and that this corruption consists of replacing them with something else without realizing what has happened. If someone, believing himself to be the pillar of religion, debases the very religion he defends, and does this in the name of religion, then that, it seems to me, is a point worth making. The fact that nothing can be done about it is quite irrelevant.

EPIGONY AND THE DEBASEMENT OF ETHICS

Finally, I want to say something about ethics and the manner in which it, too, is debased, in accordance with my law of epigony. This is a large subject, but I shall try to make my basic point briefly.

We can see this debasement, first of all, in the evolution of basic ethical terms, such as *charity, goodness,* and *virtue.* "Charity," for example, is derived from *caritas,* the Latinization of the *agape,* or Christian love of the New Testament. Originally, this was the most important ethical concept of the Christian religion. *Charity,* however, has come to mean little more than giving to the poor. Indeed, it is even common to speak of giving *to charity,* illustrating an ultimate and final corruption of a precious concept.

Similarly, the Greeks originally contrasted goodness with what is simply bad (i.e., base) and therefore by all means to be avoided in the quest for happiness or fulfillment. At the hands of moralists, however, it has come to be more or less equated with morality, such that human goodness, for example, is thought of as mere benevolence. This is, doubtless, an important human attribute, but hardly the equivalent of the idea it displaced.

The working of my law is perhaps best seen in the evolution of the concept of virtue. A virtuous man was, for the Greeks, an exceptional man, one who stood out from others by his superiority over them. Not everyone, they thought, has the capacity for virtue, and rather few ever actually achieve it. Virtue is reserved for those who are inherently better, and it must be cultivated through long training and education.

This ancient ideal of virtue, conceived as personal excellence, of rising above others by one's superiority to them as a person, was an inspiring one. It underlies every treatise of the ancient classical moralists, culminating in Aristotle's writings. But that ideal has by now become so denatured that even educated people can hardly read these great treatises without misunderstanding. Aristotle's *Nicomachean Ethics,* which is primarily concerned with the nature of virtue or individual excellence, was readily understandable to any educated Greek of his day, but not by many who undertake to read it today. Readers now suppose that, since it is a treatise on ethics, its author must be dealing with matters of right and wrong, even though those concepts do not even enter into his discussion. The concept of virtue, meanwhile, has become so trivialized that it is sometimes equated with nothing more significant than chastity. And similarly, when Aristotle refers to the *good man* we suppose him to be describing someone who respects the rights of others; who is perhaps generous, kind, and truthful in his dealings with them; and so on. Of course Aristotle meant nothing of the sort. He was thinking of the rare individual who rises above the common herd by the power of his mind; by his strength, resourcefulness, and courage; and who is therefore worth something and, in the true sense of the word, contemptuous of common people.

The manner in which this ancient ideal of human goodness came to be corrupted by those very moralists whose chief mission was to defend it was well understood by Plato. In his *Gorgias* he analyzes this decay, using Socrates' interlocutor, Callicles, as the vehicle for this analysis. The common people, Callicles notes, are a weak and mindless herd, and are very numerous. Discerning that they have no genuine virtue—that they are inferior to those exceptional few individuals who are strong and resourceful—they declare such strength and superiority not to be the marks of virtue at all. *All* men, they declare, are equal, and, as Callicles sagaciously notes, it makes these mindless masses feel very good indeed to be able to believe that they are equal to the best, and hence, just as good as they. Weakness, they declare, is not really weakness at all, but strength. Thus, Callicles notes, there arises a kind of herd morality, wherein the same words continue to be used—words like *virtue, goodness,* and *worth*—but are given meanings that are very nearly the opposite of what they originally had. And we can add to Callicles' observations that it is then only a matter of time before some religious leader will rise to strike a chord in the hearts of these wretched masses by declaring this popular ethic to be ordained by the gods themselves. It is not those who are great and noble who are blessed, he will say, but on the contrary, those who are meek, poor, and downtrodden; and it is they, he will say, whom the gods love, who are the very salt of the earth, and who will someday inherit the earth.

The cycle is thus completed, and something that is morally noble and good becomes almost totally lost sight of, replaced by something relatively worthless, this debasement being wrought, once again, by those who imagine themselves to be the upholders of morality. So great and thoroughgoing is this change that even the most thoughtful and reflective philosophers are likely to be unaware that it has even occurred. The degenerate morality becomes enshrined in custom and in popular religion, and thus comes to be taken for granted as being the true morality after all. It is very sad and, sadly, very human.

14

Priests and Prophets

Joseph L. Blau

In our society, when we use such a term as *religious professional* we tend to think of priests, ministers, and rabbis—congregational leaders— or of monastics; in other societies, *religious professional* is a broader term. It may, for example, include various types of healers. Residues of this usage remain even in our day. The prevalence of members of religious orders in such a career as nursing reminds us that graduates of medical schools still repeat *pro forma* a religious commitment, the Hippcratic Oath, as part of their graduation ceremony. There are also relics of faith-healing, both organized (as in Christian Science) and in such psychological devices as Emile Coué's popularized litany earlier in our century: "Day by day, in every way, I am getting better and better." Teaching, too, a profession that was, for a long time, a monopoly of the religious orders, still retains a monastic commitment to poverty, though the monastic commitments to chastity and to obedience have lesser weight in our time. The legal profession also has roots that bind it to earlier religious professionals, both in its mediatorial role and in the higher standards of professional morality demanded (if not always attained) by its practitioners. The element that binds all these together is that each of these professions rests upon a vast body of accumulated knowledge, passed on in ever increasing bulk through the centuries, and added to generation after generation. All of these are ways to serve humanity that demand long and often difficult preparation; they are *learned professions.*

Among the religious professionals of which the Bible speaks, there

---

Joseph L. Blau (1909–1987) was professor of religion at Columbia University.

are some who fit well into such a classification as "members of a learned profession." Some of these, akin to modern clergy, specialized in the conduct of formal sacrificial rituals, and, on biblical evidence, occasionally delivered brief sermons. Others, apparently, were official diviners, whose specialized function was the "casting of lots," that is to say, determining which possible royal action in a given situation was "the will of God." We do not know precisely what was involved; it has been suggested that the jewels in the breastplate of the high priest were used, possibly in a procedure like the rolling of dice. Other priests were physicians and lawyers. There were probably some who were architects, for the Bible preserves a certain amount of detail about the plan of the temple. We read of sacred musicians and singers, who had roles in the processions that were intrinsic features of the temple services. Even the artisans who made the sacred vessels for use in the shrine must have been part of this religious "caste." Otherwise, either their work would not have been used in the temple or they would themselves have been "smitten" for touching sacred materials or objects.

All that precluded the maintenance of a strict monopoly of religion by this group of official religious professionals, whose development and expansion is hinted in the Bible and whose function was to carry on the state religion, was the simultaneous—and occasionally overlapping—existence of another type of religious figure, the seer or prophet. Some prophets, like Ezekiel, came from priestly families, but saw "visions," and were for that reason counted among the prophets. "And I looked, and, behold a whirlwind came out of the north, a great cloud, and a fire unfolding itself, and a brightness was about it. . . . This was the appearance of the likeness of the glory of the Lord. . . ." Others, like Amos, a herdsman, were explicitly against the rituals of the official cult, and, as we all do, ascribed his own view to God: "I hate, I despise your feast days,/ And I will not smell in your solemn assemblies./ Though ye offer me burnt offerings and your meat offerings, I will not accept them:/ . . . But let judgment run down as waters,/ And righteousness as a mighty stream" (chap. 5). Jeremiah heard "The word that came . . . from the Lord," and called upon all the nations to heed his words and "Hear the word of the Lord, O ye nations" (chap. 31). Isaiah "saw words" (chap. 2) and also "saw the Lord sitting upon a throne" and "heard the voice of the Lord" (chap. 6).

Each prophet presented his prophecy as a message directly from God to the king, or to the cultic authorities, or to the people, or even to an enemy country. In the final analysis, their inspired task was to tell them all what they did *not* want to hear in times of well-being and prosperity, and to comfort all in times of adversity with the assurance that God was still on the side of His people. Put another way, the prophets spoke for the supremacy of God over the state and its institutions, including those of the official religion. In contrast, the priests are presented (by the prophets) as speaking for the supremacy of the state and its institutions, including the official cult, over the people.

Thus the scriptural text presents two versions of religious nationalism: a "priestly" patriotism expressed by adherence to the dictates of the king, sanctified by the priests (especially the "high priest") and imposed upon the people; and a "prophetic" patriotism founded upon the spiritual insight of continued divine activity, concern, and guidance. Each of the two versions asserted its own divine authority: the "priestly" rule was referred to a divine law once revealed; the "prophetic" word was claimed as new and direct revelation from on high, often superseding or reinterpreting the earlier law.

I have, perhaps, seemed to exaggerate the difference. Certainly Judaism and Christianity—both of which are later variants of Hebrew religion—have made every effort, even as did the compilers of the biblical text, to de-emphasize, even to dismiss completely, the differences between "priest" and "prophet." In deference to biblical scholarship, I have chosen here to speak of "priestly" and "prophetic," and to use these adjectives to indicate differing modes of approach that still show through the scriptural text shared by Jews and Christians. My further contention is that both modes are still prevalent in our world, and perhaps especially in our country today, and that each mode, in its own way, can be beneficial, but operating together they are a bane.

An instance or two may demonstrate the difference between a "priestly" and a "prophetic" outlook. We might begin with Aaron, the priest, leading the sacrificial worship of the golden calf (Exod. 32) while Moses, his "brother" the prophet, communed with the deity on the mountain top, but this is too plainly a mythical statement to serve as the basis for a scholarly paper. More directly relevant, though conceivably as mythical, is the story of the divine chastisement announced to King David by Nathan the prophet, because of David's dubious dealings in the matter of Bathsheba and her husband, Uriah the Hittite (2 Samuel 11–12). In David's time, however, the temple had not been built; it is doubtful whether the large priestly bureaucracy that the temple and its activities required was yet in place.

International relations in Solomon's time when the temple was built were solidified in the common fashion of monarchs the world over, even in our day, by mutiple marriages into the ruling families of other lands. Thus Solomon became a by-word for the number of his alliances—and of his brides. Each bride, however, brought with her not only her retainers and her handmaidens, but also her gods. So, from the early days of the monarchy, the temple of the iconic Yahweh was graced by idols representing the "strange gods" of Solomon's wives. There is no record of a "priestly" protest in Solomon's reign or in any later reign. Good diplomacy, we might say, outweighed bad religion. In later days, when the great "prophetic" era began, many cried out against such concessions to the foreign wives of the kings of both Judah and Israel, and proclaimed this usage responsible for the revenge that Yahweh took upon the people. For Yahweh was a "jealous god."

Again, in the various historical books of the Bible, we note the "priestly" emphasis on animal sacrifice as a means of atonement for the sins of humanity, both collective and individual. In the books attributed to the prophets, such sacrifices are played down, and, in some cases, decried and denounced. "Prophetic" emphasis is placed on repentance and reformation. Atonement is an internal moral matter; animal sacrifice is, at best, an outward sign of repentance. It is in a "prophetic" text (Micah 6) that we read: "He hath shewed you, O man, what is good;/ and what doth the Lord require of thee,/ But to do justly and to love mercy,/ And to walk humbly with thy God?" And, in the "prophetic" text of Hosea (chapter 6), God speaks: "I desired mercy, and not sacrifice; and the knowledge of God more than burnt offerings. But they like men have transgressed the covenant:/ There have they dealt treacherously against me."

In the "prophetic" books appears, too, the notion that the divine election of the children of Israel carries with it special moral responsibility rather than special privilege: "You only have I known of all the families of the earth: Therefore I will punish you for all your iniquities" (Amos 3). "Prophetic" morality (then, as now) tended to see current moral behavior in decline. The people, and especially the rich, had degenerated. The land owners oppressed the farmers, the city dwellers feasted on the labor of the country folk; the homely virtue of olden times fell victim to urban luxury, gluttony, adultery; worst of all, the government and the servile priesthood, in their foreign policies, fawned on the larger powers, often adopting alien deities (see, especially, the "parable" of Aholah-Samaria, and Aholilah-Jerusalem, Ezek. 23; also Isa. 29 and 30), which the prophets associated with whoring.

If the prophetic books show little respect for the priests, seeing in them only those who increased their power by flattering the king and catering to the worst impulses of the people, the priestly powers had as little regard for the prophetic expressions. Moreover, from time to time, in both the books of Kings and the books of Chronicles, it is apparent that a considerable part of the population of the country cared not at all for either the priests or the prophets of Yahweh. The people worshipped, rather, (if they worshipped at all) the ancient *baalim,* the nature-deities, and other popular gods of a basically rural agricultural population. That much is clear even in the books of Kings as we have them. The "high places" at which the people carried on their worship "were not removed: the people sacrificed and burned incense still in the high places" (2 Kings 15). Yet Jotham, the son of Uzziah who reigned over Judah at this time, "did that which was right in the sight of the Lord"—one of the rare monarchs of whom that was said. Jotham's son and successor Ahaz "walked in the way of the kings of Israel," who were, for the most part, pagans. Ahaz "sacrificed and burnt incense in the high places, and on the hills, and under every green tree" (2 Kings 16). He even ordered the priest Urijah to build a new altar in the temple in a design copied from one he had seen at Damascus, an order which Urijah carried out (2 Kings 16). Meanwhile things were no better in the northern kingdom, where Hoshea the son of Elah became king in the twelfth year of the reign of Ahaz in Judah. Hoshea's capital city of Samaria was captured and his people carried away into Assyrian capitvity. Hosea himself "did that which was evil in the sight of the Lord" though not as badly as his predecessors. The loss to Assyria came about because "the children of Israel had sinned . . . and walked in the statutes of the heathen . . . and . . . did secretly those things that were not right . . . and they built themselves high places in all their cities . . ." and so forth (2 Kings 17).

I shall not take the time to add to this suggestive inquiry into priestly and prophetic differences a further inquiry into the reasons some of the prophets—those whose "words of the Lord" did not agree with the "words of the Lord" proclaimed by Isaiah, Jeremiah, Amos, Ezekiel, and others, but did, generally, agree with the royal and priestly views—are referred to as "false prophets." We are aware that the "heroes" of the past, and the "villains" of the past, are so called by their successors, not by their contemporaries. The Old Testament, as we have it, is an *ex post facto* narrative, not an eyewitness report.

It is more to the point of our session to take note that we are today, in the United States, living through a period reminiscent in many ways of the biblical era of kings and priests, and of many prophets, some of whom will be called "false" by our descendants. If we reflect, for a moment, on the history of the United States, we shall see that, while religion was undoubtedly a shaping force in the colonial era, the type of religion in most of the colonies was more "prophetic" than "priestly," especially during and after the Great Awakening of the early eighteenth century. The "priestly" forces, as a general rule, both in the eighteenth and nineteenth centuries, distrusted the type of religiosity promoted by the "prophetic," "revivalistic" religious groups. One can easily understand why in the 1790s, at the time of the Second Great Awakening, it has been said that a mere ten percent of the population were church members. A far larger proportion expressed its religious impulses in intense, though infrequent, revivals.

This pattern of preferring "prophetic" evangelical revivalism to church membership persisted, though in less extreme proportions through the nineteenth century and into the twentieth. The urban masses of immigrants from abroad, or internal migrants in times of economic crisis, were especially good subjects for revivalistic attention. As late as my own boyhood, in the early 1920s, Billy Sunday's evangelical revival came to New York City, put up a big tent on a vacant lot at 168th Street and Broadway (where now the Columbia-Presbyterian Medical Center is located), drew large crowds, and a good deal of resentful comment by the "regular" clergy in the city. More recent, and stylistically more contemporary, evangelists have continued to find many nonchurch-goers susceptible to radio and television quasi-prophetic, individualistic, stagey revivalism, while many churches find it hard to manage bare survival.

Nor can this contemporary preference for "prophetic," emotional religiosity over a necessarily more and more "priestly" intellectual defense of faith be attributed to the absence of a religious establishment in the United States. In Great Britain, too, the established Church of England is losing its membership to the point at which those churches that have completely lost their flocks have to receive support. A recent feature in the *Manchester Guardian Weekly* (September 14, 1986, p. 20: "A Country Diary," by Roger A. Redfern) spoke of the "Stockwood Church, abandoned now but preserved beside its ancient yew by the Redundant Churches Fund." Without governmental subsidies, our "redundant churches" in the United States may be used for other purposes, sacred or not, or they may become evangelical shrines where perpetual revivals are led by entrepreneurial, evangelical "prophets." Echoes of this revolt against rational religion can be found in colleges and universities, from the backwoods populist ones to the most elite; in governmental bureaus and business offices; in Hollywood and its suburb, Washington—indeed, everywhere in America.

Here, in conclusion, I must return to the matter that I barely mentioned before. There were "true prophets" and "false prophets" in the Old Testament narratives, and the different adjectival attributions could be made only after the fact. A "true prophet" is one whose prophecies "came true"; a "false prophet" is one whose prophecies "proved false." If the churches and other instrumentalities of rational religion can become the commonplaces of the religions of the next century, then those who so prophesy will be known as the "true prophets" of our time. This rational religion would be one that has come to terms with our modern knowledge of physical science and social science; one that recognizes that human life and its conditions and restrictions change with the increase of knowledge; one that admits, without defensive hedging, that its profoundest doctrines are figures of speech, not demonstrable truths; one that accepts that here is not a fixed set of ultimate values, but that humankind in its evolutionary development creates penultimate values for each epoch as it unfolds out of human life. If, on the other hand, a nostalgic evangelism, such as is today epidemic in our country, should prevail, then those of us who detest its coming, abhor its anti-intellectualism, and feel confident that the American people are too sane to hold to it for the long run—we optimists will be proved to have been the "false prophets" of our age.

15

Reason and Ethics

Joseph Fletcher

Hamlet, mad as a hatter, nevertheless says to Rosencrantz and Guilden-stern—I think in the second act—"There is nothing right or wrong but thinking makes it so." And it is precisely that, I think, which we have in mind. In order really to do any kind of rational, ethical analysis of human conduct, and make any intelligible rationalizations in general about human conduct, we have to think. And, of course, religious ethics, like religious thinking in general, rejects any notion of moral thought-fulness and insists on a humble, obedient following of normative rules of conduct, which have been gained by them, either by divine com-mandments and revelation or by some kind of ecclesiastical inference from human experience.

I propose to be relatively brief, making essentially three points. It is rather easy, as a matter of fact, to pull Scripture apart in terms of its internal contradictions and errors. After all, biblical ethics itself is only ascribed to by one of a great number of religions because, by definition, religion is capable of indefinite variables and variations.

First, ethics may be either secular or religious, depending on the presuppositions of a given system of theory. The second point is that religion distorts the principles and reasoning employed in ethics. And the third point is this: The heart of the issue is the metaethical belief that undergirds religious ethics; namely, that right and wrong are already given to us in an objective moral order and our human task is not to *determine* what is right and wrong but to *discover* what is.

Joseph Fletcher is professor emeritus of medical ethics, University of Virginia Medical School.

SECULAR OR RELIGIOUS ETHICS

Any ethics—any theory about ethics and the moral practice following from that theory—takes its true identity from its metaethics, that is, its presuppositions, its *Weltanschauung,* its world view, all that is pre-supposed in the moral ruminations of the thoughtful man or woman. A major difference in this respect is that lying right at the very heart of secular and scientific thinking is a way of looking at life and experience in terms of empirical data, of what is possibly verifiable, and certainly what should be falsifiable if untrue. And all of the cognitive limitations of human knowledge, the kind of intellectual humility that is characteristic of scientific inquiry and genuine investigation on the one hand, stands over against the religious or speculative way of looking at life and experience in terms of ethical assertions, faith assertions, about transcendental entities that are by definition either verifiable or falsifiable.

The case for, or defense of, ethical autonomy—that is, that moral philosophy can stand on its own human feet without God or a deity or a religious belief—is well established in scientific and philosophical circles, and even some religious thinkers nowadays tend to concede that ethical autonomy is a tenable position to take. Aristotle's *Nicomachean Ethics* is still, in our own day, taken seriously as though the Middle Ages had never intervened. On the streets and in the villages, however, it is commonly supposed that morality and religion go together like the horse and carriage, and recently the Brookings Institution, which is a profit-making think tank in Washington, D.C., released a report entitled "Religion in American Public Life" in which the conclusion was that the stability of society depends on the underpinnings of religion. Through religion, the report said, human rights are rooted in the moral worth with which our loving creator has endowed each human soul, and social authority is legitimized by making it answerable to a transcendental moral law. Now, of course, there was an immediate outcry of protest but, just the same, that report reflects a deeply rooted, visceral sentiment—the religious sentiment. And the case of secular humanism cuts right across what Paul Kurtz, in his book *The Transcendental Temptation,* calls the schizoid nature of human beings: one part of us hungers for myths that transcend our finite existence, and the other part is rational, practical, and intellectually humble. Most of us would say with Paul Camus that we are willing to live with what we know, and that is an essential piece of intellectual humility necessary to any kind of creative reasoning.

My own judgment is that this tendency to religiousness will continue to be the human condition. It will always be around. As a humanist, I will settle for the clear evidence, so it seems to me, that in a democratic society, the medieval part of us is being denied by a growing norm, accepted even by some religionists—namely, that private and personal mystical beliefs may not be imposed on others or on the public will.

HOW RELIGION DISTORTS

Coherent religious believers, and there are some, trace their ethics to either what God commands (shown in Revelation), or on what they infer from what they believe to be the divine nature and being. Let us look at the ethics of treatment of grossly defective newborns as a case in point.

I know a religious ethicist who holds that we may never morally withhold life-saving treatment or let such tragic creatures die, because to do so is involuntary euthanasia and, as such, is forbidden by a moral rule, a universal prohibition coming from God. Leaving aside the actual problem of such decisions—and they are very grievous—see how religion is twisting things. Those in the religious camp always describe the rest of us as mere consequentialists, because we try to determine what is right and wrong by the foreseeable consequences of a given course of action, measured by human benefit. What they hold is in fact consequentialist too, only theirs are the consequences that they believe to be entailed in the next world, the world that they believe in, and what, therefore, we might call a kind of eschatological consequentialism. If pressed hard enough, they will admit that their moral choice is determined by God's approval of their obedience to His (note His) rulings against euthanasia, which He will reward in the after life, rather than caring about the earthly human consequences for that tragic baby, for it's family, and for it's community.

Here we can see a distortion of the values that are at stake in that kind of tragic decision-making. Religionists hold to the alleged sanctity of life rather than to a critical and thoughtful quality of life standard. But also we can see the distortion of the very concept of consequences. This is genuine intellectual distortion. For all their rejection of consequential ethics, believers in fact are consequentialists, but in terms of a highly mythical/mystical ideology. And the end result is something that humanists, with their worldly outlook, could not possibly buy.

METAETHICS

The creationist doctrine of religious believers, which attributes the world and its natural causes to a divine initiative, entails, either by direct revelation or by inference, the belief that God's will is the source and sanction of morality. Or, in another kind of rhetoric, religionists hold that right and wrong are grounded firmly in an objective moral order set right into the very nature of things, *de rerum natura*. And on this foundation, it follows, logically, that for religious believers the problem of man's moral life is to discover what is right and what is wrong, not to decide what is right and what is wrong. Revelation or religious inference theologically supply us, the religionists think, with the moral principles of a sovereign and eternal God; they are rules of universal obligation, not merely generalizations about what we ought or ought not to do. There is no place in their scheme of things—in the religious scheme of things—for variables in situations, allowing sometimes for what is disallowed at other times.

When Shakespeare's Hamlet said what I quoted at the beginning of this discussion, he was, whether intentionally or not, emphasizing the importance of human beings deciding about right and wrong and not simply adhering to moral rules, which, by their preemptive authority, eliminate the moral agent altogether because he has nothing to do but follow the rules, and conscience becomes increasingly irrelevant.

Those are my three points, put very barely, for the sake of discussion. Let me close with a recommendation. I dare to make this as an octogenarian who has seen something of both sides of the issue between secular and religious outlooks. I want to urge humanists to define their way of looking at the world negatively, not positively. That is, it should be understood to be a nontheist outlook, not a blank affirmation of human beings. Mark Twain was a self-styled humanist and still he could say to his friend William Dean Howells, "You know, I think there have never been more than 1,800 people in the world that I'd sit down to have lunch with." Surrounded as we are with human prejudice and timidities and selfishness and violence and thoughtlessness, both individually and collectively, nobody, I would say, with an ounce of intelligence is going to be sentimental enough to like people a lot of the time. We've all read and heard humanists talk in panegyrics about human beings. Lincoln used to call it balderdash. I hope that as far as human beings go, humanists will rank them first among the anthropoids and tops in the evolutionary order, but I also hope that they will define their position as humanists—as those who do without godtalk and godthought, avoiding any appearance of putting people in the place that God has in religious beliefs and religious heads. In short, humanist idolatry is as silly as theist idolatry, and arguably even sillier.

Epilogue

Paul Kurtz

The theme of this conference is very important. It ought to be debated more than it is. The reason we decided to have this conference on biblical versus secular ethics is that the Bible has become a center of controversy in America today: it is used for political and moral reasons. Unfortunately, its premises are never questioned. There are millions of Americans who believe that all of morality and all of ethics must be grounded in absolute biblical truth; that any other point of view is immoral, sinful, and wicked. They believe that without a Bible-based morality, there can be no ethical obligation or responsibility. This is the very question that secularists and humanists want to debate.

This is *Free Inquiry* magazine's fifth conference. It is co-sponsored by our Committee for the Scientific Examination of Religion and our Biblical Criticism Research Project, both of which use the very best scientific, critical, and scholarly techniques available to examine the Bible, and religion in general; to examine religious claims openly and objectively without any presuppositions. Our first conference, on "Science, the Bible, and Darwin," was held at the State University of New York at Buffalo in 1982. The second, in 1983, was on "Religion and Politics" and held at the National Press Club in Washington, D.C. The third conference, on "Armageddon and Biblical Apocalyptic," was held in 1984 at the University of Southern California. Last year, "Jesus in History and Myth," an historic conference in many ways, was held at the University of Michigan in Ann Arbor.

The present conference, on biblical versus secular ethics, has historic

Paul Kurtz is professor of philosophy at the State University of New York at Buffalo and editor of *Free Inquiry* magazine.

implications in that there are millions of good citizens in this country who believe in the Bible, but their belief is never examined critically, objectively, and impartially.

America, and much of the world, is going through moral change— moral convulsions of a sort—and rapid social change. Part of this results from widespread dispute about the basis of morality and how we want to live, a confrontation that has profound ramifications and about which we hear new stories emerging every day. There are those who believe that ethics must be absolute, that all ethical principles and rules must be divinely inspired, that they are given from God, and that the be-all and end-all of ethical wisdom is summed up in the New and Old Testaments. These moral absolutists attempt to use this point of view to either stop social change or to bring about a different kind of social change. The Bible is thus used as a weapon, one that is being used powerfully against the schools.

In the Mobile, Alabama, textbook case, people claimed that the textbooks undermined the morality of America's children and that they violated the principles of the Bible. At present, there is a massive confrontation all over this land about the extent to which biblical morality and the biblical point of view ought to be taught. Much the same kind of attack is being made in the courts themselves with respect to judicial appointees. It is a radical view by people who want to move away from a secular republic, people who believe that this is a Judeo-Christian society and that legal interpretations, legal constraints, ought to be based in some sense on the Bible. There is a profound critique of the mass media and the publishing industry in America from the same forces. Many of these advocates use the Bible as the basis for foreign policy, for interpreting events in the world, and how to deal with other nations that may disagree with us. Lastly, moral absolutism is being used to seize political control. It is no secret that one of the aspirants in that direction lives in the State of Virginia.

Thus, we are forced to debate the Bible, whether we want to do so or not. It is not considered polite in many circles to question fundamental religious assumptions, and the Bible has not been considered a book that could be read critically and objectively. Either you are for it or against it. Most people approach it in a rather propagandistic mode. The real task is to convert believers and to awaken faith and conviction. It seems to me that the Bible, because of its political, moral, and social implications, remains relevant in America today. When I go to Europe and meet my many colleagues, they are dismayed at this fact. People in England or Holland or France are surprised at the fact the Bible has become so important again, because in many intellectual circles these issues were debated centuries ago and are no longer socially relevant.

In the present context of the American debate, what is not appreciated is that there are other sources of morality besides the Bible. That seems so obvious to those who are part of the university culture. Nonetheless, there is an abysmal ignorance in the United States. People do not appreciate the fact that Western civilization has Greco-Roman origins, that the great philosophers—Aristotle, Socrates, Epicurus, Marcus Aurelius, Spinoza, Kant, Mill, down through the twentieth century—have been concerned with ethical questions, and that there has been an effort to base ethics on practical wisdom and to develop an ethic of excellence and nobility. There has been a profound concern within secular culture, throughout the entire history of civilization, to deal with the problems of social justice and the needs of others. It is a surprise, indeed a shock, to learn from many citizens today that unless a biblically based ethic is accepted, then morality has no foundation.

The Greco-Roman secular basis for morality has come to fruition in the Renaissance and the Enlightenment, with the dawn of modern science and the development of the democratic revolutions, and has been the basis for the whole modernistic trend. Certainly, we do have a Judeo-Christian background, and of course, we appreciate it. We appreciate the fact that the Bible is a book of literary excellence, moral insight, and moral wisdom. On the other hand, many of us are aware of the fact that the Bible is not the final word on ethical choices. It does not help us, for example, in medical ethics, one of the rapidly changing fields of today. It does not help us deal with people from other cultures who view the world from diverse religious backgrounds. Though the Bible was written 1900–3000 years ago by a nomadic and agricultural people, and expressed the moral outlook and perspective of its time, it is surprising to think that the Bible could be stretched entirely and used absolutely for a post-modern, technological, urbanized society such as ours. The scholars here assembled examine the Bible and find much that is meritorious, but also, no doubt, they point out contradictions and difficulties in interpretation. We think that the Bible ought to be debated. It is not currently being debated, and that has been our purpose. We think the Bible should be read—as any other book is read—in light of the best scientific, philosophical, linguistic, and historical techniques of scholarship.